MW01098679

THE ONE-MINUTE
FINANCIAL
PLANNER

THE ONE-MINUTE FINANCIAL PLANNER

Common Misconceptions People Hold About
Money, Investing, and Retirement

JOEL T. REDMOND, CFP ®

Copyright © 2011 by Joel T. Redmond, CFP ®.

Library of Congress Control Number:		2011902040
ISBN:	Hardcover	978-1-4568-6645-7
	Softcover	978-1-4568-6644-0
	Ebook	978-1-4568-6646-4

All rights reserved. No part of this book may be reproduced or transmitted in any form or by any means, electronic or mechanical, including photocopying, recording, or by any information storage and retrieval system, without permission in writing from the copyright owner.

This book was printed in the United States of America.

To order additional copies of this book, contact:
Xlibris Corporation
1-888-795-4274
www.Xlibris.com
Orders@Xlibris.com
94052

TABLE OF CONTENTS

- A diversified portfolio of no-loads is enough; I'll be OK with that. Fees are for fools.
- All the market data is garbage; they only use backward-looking data.
- Just buy low P/E stocks and rebalance annually.
- I watch Bloomberg and read the financial press.
- I use stop-loss orders.
- This stock *has* to go up, because (insert fundamental/business reason here).
- I can time the market.
- Fire your broker the first time she lags the benchmark.
- Bargains don't exist anymore in the markets.
- Asset allocation doesn't work anymore.

- I should always convert my traditional IRA to a Roth IRA.
- Tax-free bonds are enough.
- I'll never get audited.
- My CPA knows everything.
- My CPA doesn't know *anything*.
- Taxes are a curse on any free society.
- Quickbooks is enough.
- A gain I have to pay taxes on is worse than no gain at all.
- I've got the expenses in my head.
- I'm taking as much as I can under the table.

- I'm taking my Social Security at 62; it won't even be there when I'm 70.
- Annuities are too expensive.
- Annuities are too hard to understand.
- Always take the lump sum in a pension plan, not the annuity.
- I'll work until I die. Why do I really need a plan?
- My own company's plan is as good as anything else when I retire. Why move the money?

- I don't mind a lower interest rate as long as I don't lose my principal.
- I have a retirement plan. I got it from (existing advisor, online, discount firm staff, etc.).
- I've done my plan. Isn't that enough?
- It'll all be gone and I don't even want to look at it. Why bother?

- I don't need an estate plan.
- I'll leave it all to my spouse.
- We have everything titled jointly.
- I don't want to think about dying.
- My kids can't handle the money. Leave them out.
- My kids are well off. I don't need a plan.
- I have a revocable living trust.
- I'll gift later on, just before I go.
- It's safer under the mattress; I don't want my heirs knowing anything.
- I did my will on nolo.com. All set.

For JB, and for Frank, who has always been extraordinary

FOREWORD

TO THIS DAY, my father still occasionally complains that I never learned two things in high school—Latin and computer. (I went to private school.) But there were lots of other things there I never learned that he never complained about. Among them were:

- How a stock differs from a bond
- How GDP is calculated
- How governments influence and set interest rates
- How the American credit system works

And dozens of others tied to finance. What's more worrisome than never having learned these things is having it not occur to parents to change this dilemma. Why are we like this? In part, the answer lies in our inability (or unwillingess) to weave personal finance into the fabric of the American school system. At least, not consistently, not yet.

This book is *not* designed as a text for those classrooms. If you try and use it that way, you'll be disappointed. There are many scholarly works out there that can fill that gap very well. What this book *is* designed to do is give the average person, who may or may not have received formal instruction in finance, a point of departure for approaching their own financial lives more intelligently. The book is divided into six general segments, which correspond to the six areas of practice for professional financial planners. Each section is then subdivided into ten common misconceptions that arise in these fields. Some are misconceptions I encountered (and still encounter) in my own financial planning practice. Some are misconceptions that I've heard other planners or clients bring up. A few are the result of my attempts to sit on the other side of the desk, where the clients sit, and think of what I'd be afraid to say to the person across from me.

Many students learn relatively complex things in high school—differential and integral calculus, inorganic chemistry, computer programming, foreign languages. Few of them, however, learn practicable lessons that can affect them as much as a working knowledge of personal finance. It's my hope that readers of this book, having gotten a taste of the field, will become excited enough to implement some of these concepts in their own lives, with or without a paid professional to help them.

JOEL T. REDMOND, CFP ®

FINANCIAL PLANNING

The misconception:

I DON'T NEED a financial plan. They're 200 pages and incomprehensible.

The reality:

Every investor already has a plan, whether consciously developed and written down or not. The best possible thing for any investor who can (and in some cases, can't) meet current obligations and bills is to develop a well-thought out and executable financial plan.

The proof:

Go outside and take a walk down your street. On any given street on any given day in America, the odds are that you'll see a variety of buildings—homes, businesses, skyscrapers. Literally none of them—not a single one—was crafted without a plan, a set of drawings and estimates used to create them. The basic steps in building a house are more visible, perhaps, than a financial plan for an investor. The foundation must be dug—a hole in the ground has to be cleared. Cement has to get poured down in the right mixture, at the right level, in the appropriate amount of time. The foundation has to be laid—the beams and support that keep the entire house from collapsing in storm, rain, snow and wind. The electrical and heating and plumbing systems have to be built. The roof and windows and floors have to be sheet rocked and painted and shingled and tarred and sided. And so forth.

The same analogy works for any investor. With a few happy exceptions of individuals who seem to do nothing but work and therefore have far more disposable income than they can use, most people need to know how to manage their wealth and how to continue managing that wealth! Typically, any plan should address the needs of the investor, the goals of the investor, and the priorities of the investor. Just as you don't give candy out at Christmas to those who haven't gotten a meal, neither should someone who has significant credit problems be seduced by hints of amassing rapid wealth in the markets with the proverbial "hot stock."

The dictionary definition of a plan, as used in financial planning, is "a formal program for specified needs, benefits, etc. : *a pension plan.*" (Dictionary.com) In this sense, any investor who has a formal program for defining what he or she wants to accomplish financially has a plan. Formal implies that the plan is usually written; and it is true that many plans are dozens to even hundreds of pages in length. Investors with many moving parts to their financial machinery require more pages in their plan. The most important point, however, remains: has a result been specified? Has a goal been determined? Have there been parameters set? Will the investor accomplish the goals if he or she implements the plan? If not, what chance does he or she have for accomplishing this? Finally, what happens if the goals are not met?

The Board for Financial Planning Standards defines financial planning as "the process of whether and how an individual can meet life goals through the proper management of financial resources." (Mershon, *Fundamentals of Personal Financial Planning.*) This plan does not need to be written; however, the odds are that the plan's perceived effectiveness and trustworthiness will be proportional to its formality.

This definition is revealing; the first step is for the client to decide what they want! Many clients view financial planning as a psychological lift, or merely an excuse to go and visit an elegant office and feel important discussing minutiae with ambitious and conscientious people in suits. Most investors, however, have recognized the need for sound financial planning, particularly in light of the terrifying 2008 market "mini-Depression."

Many firms have different styles of plans. Merrill Lynch, traditionally the leading "wirehouse" brokerage form in America, has historically used a leatherbound, 100+ page volume prepared for clients called "The Financial Foundation." Some of the smaller independent agents use one page summaries of specific actions a client and advisor are to mutually take; many financial planners will agree that it doesn't matter whether it's written on a napkin or a detailed Excel report, so long as it works and the client does it!

To do:

- Find a financial planner. You can locate one in your area by going onto www/cfp.net/search and looking by name or ZIP code.
- Check the planner's record by entering his/her name into FINRA's BrokerCheck. This will tell you if the planner has had any disciplinary actions against them, as well as what they were. http://www.finra.org/Investors/ToolsCalculators/BrokerCheck/
- Call one of the planners and inquire about their practice. See what type of clients they serve and if they'll meet with you for a free consultation or if you can obtain a free plan. Make sure you know what the fees are (if there are any) before you book a meeting.

The misconception:

The cheapest product wins; there are too many choices.

The reality:

Precisely because there are so many choices, the selection of the right person is likely the most important decision the would-be successful investor has to make, whatever fees are paid.

The proof:

The first official mutual fund was MFS Investors Trust, released in 1924. The fund held 45 different securities, including 10 shares of U.S. Steel, 5 shares of General Electric (at $232.50!) and 50 shares of General Motors. Fast forward to 2011, and the choices are staggering. Over 8,000 mutual funds sold in the US were listed with the Investment Company Institute as of October 2007. Two years later, a search through Bloomberg revealed over 23,000 choices for open-ended mutual fund choices. CFA Institute estimates that there are 48,000 open-ended mutual funds worldwide.

And funds are only one type of security available on our markets. Investors can choose from over 2,300 publicly traded stocks on the NYSE, and over 2,800 more on the NASDAQ. They can also trade in any of the other securities trading on regional exchanges like those in Boston, Chicago, or Philadelphia. An estimated 15,000 equity securities comprise most of the volume for these trades; much of this volume comes from additional issues in the over-the-counter (OTC) and Pink Sheet (penny stock) markets.

Then there are options. Of the S & P 500, for example, 499 companies have options sold on them—puts and calls with varying dates and exercise prices. Each of these derivative securities has its own symbol and trades in a free market, adding thousands of additional securities to the mix.

Then there are the bond markets—municipal, government, and corporate. The unprecedented debt issuance in the past 3 years has made many investors skeptical of government debt issuances, but there have been bright spots—for example, the Build America Bond program incepted by President Obama in April 2009. From then until February 2010 alone, these taxable municipal bonds amounted to over $78 billion in capital projects financing, helping pay for improvements on everything from the UCLA school district to the Triborough Bridge. Investors pay tax on the interest from the bonds, but the rates are typically higher, paying up to 6-7.5% in some cases.

The additional choices offer such a monetary mélange that it's impossible to even begin to describe them: fixed, variable and equity-indexed annuities; CDs, money market funds and other cash equivalents; the various structured products that many brokerage houses offer as an incentive to their larger clients; and the increasingly interconnected world of commodities, currencies, interest rates, indices, and futures on them. Finally, the estimated 10,000 players in the hedge fund industry, as well as the private offerings listed, make it impossible to determine the total number of securities available at any time.

So how does an investor know what to do? Basically, three questions have to be answered. 1. Do you want to do it yourself, or do you want to work with someone else? 2. If you want to work with someone else, do you know that they know more than you do? 3. Does that person have a process by which he or she works that intuitively satisfies your requirements? Does

JOEL T. REDMOND, CFP ®

talking with this person give you a good gut feeling? These are the starting points to deal with.

If you feel you'd like to hire someone, try and find someone who may work with a friend or family member. Many people confide more in their financial planner than they do their significant other—there's a lot of trust that develops! Ask the planner what area they specialize in and how their process works. If they don't have one or they strike you as someone who shoots from the hip, keep looking! It's process, not product, that provides success to individual investors in today's exceedingly volatile markets. If your advisor isn't disciplined enough to set a course with you and help you stay on it, you may never get to your destination!

If you're going to go it alone, do your homework. Read the works of people who have practiced financial planning and investment management for a living. Go to seminars and educational workshops. Learn how to "read" fundamental research and the basics of charting and technical work. Most of all, make sure you never risk more in investments than you can afford to lose, and that you have an adequate understanding of your time horizon—the amount of time between now and when you'll begin to need accessing your money.

For those who wish to do it themselves, here are a few pointers:

The most important decision you will make is to decide your time horizon—i.e., how long you'll invest for. I won't give a specific rule here, but I will say that there is generally a direct relationship between the amount of time you'll stay invested and the percentage of your portfolio you'll want to invest in stocks. Less time, less in stocks. More time, more in stocks.

The second major decision is to know how much of your money you wouldn't mind losing—i.e. your risk capital. If you're unafraid of losing everything, you can invest everything in equities. If you wouldn't mind losing a third, invest a third in equities, and so on.

The third decision is how much to allocate between the four major asset classes—stocks, bonds, currencies, and commodities. Those wishing for a better understanding of the relationship between these assets would do well to consult John J. Murphy's *Intermarket Analysis: Profiting from Global*

Market Relationships. Simply getting a better grasp on the relationship between these four asset classes will help almost anyone become a better investor.

A final point: the fee isn't everything. The goal is what matters. I've had clients who paid very high fees and were ecstatic, and I've had others who paid almost nothing but will call irate about a nominal sum for account management, etc. The best clients in any field are the ones that really have a problem, that communicate it to the professional, and that the professional can solve well by what she does. Clients want to make sure their advisors are paid when they do their jobs well. They expect to. Fees do eat into an account over time, but the client won't look back at the end of their life counting the cost of their planner. They'll be gauging their success on how close they came to their dreams. Perhaps a significant investment in a planner that is committed to that is worth a hundred times the fee paid.

To do:

- Find a friend, family member, or acquaintance in the financial services industry and ask if they know where you can get your hands on a Series 7 exam course book or outline. Typically these courses are taught at vocational colleges like Bryant & Stratton, Kaplan University, and industry-specific providers like the Securities Industry Association and Securities Training Corporation. They provide the same level of knowledge that a typical registered representative entering the industry has and provide a very good overview of the products available.
- Create a checklist of questions you want answered to gauge the level of knowledge of any rep you're thinking of working with. If you don't want to create one yourself, use this one: http://www.pueblo.gsa.gov/cic_text/money/financial-planner/10questions.html
- Go onto your community's daily/weekly newspaper's website and look through the events calendar. Search for a financial services seminar of some type and attend it.

The misconception:

I have a plan. My broker did one for me.

JOEL T. REDMOND, CFP ®

The reality:

Creating a plan, while a good start, is only the first step on the journey to creating a financially sound future. Implementation and constant monitoring of the plan on an ongoing basis are the other (oft-forgotten) critical steps.

The proof:

The CFP Board's 2009 Study on Consumer Personal Finance indicated that 17% of investors surveyed had a financial plan that was regularly updated. An additional 8% had a financial plan but had not had it updated in the past year, 11% had had a plan at some time past but no active plan now, and 64% had no plan at all.

This is unconscionable. 2008 was the worst year for capital markets since 1932. An investor putting money into the Dow Jones Industrial Average at the all-time market high of 14,159.62, on 10.9.07, would still have been down 16.50% as of press time—over three years later. The sequence of returns problem, which obtains when investors experience negative returns at the beginning of systematic withdrawals from retirement accounts, would have magnified these losses and possibly deprived investors of half their account balances in a single calendar year.

At the same time, the dizzying pace of change in the financial and securities field itself gives investors pause. Bernie Madoff was able to deceive some of the most powerful people in business—Steven Spielberg, Kevin Bacon, the trustees of Yeshiva University—as well as the humbler groups of electrical workers, carpenters, and thousands of other skilled professionals. Some lost up to 90% of their pensions because of investments with the fraudulent fund. On the heels of this deception, as well as the wrenching upheaval in the residential real estate, credit, and equity markets, comes an increasingly hostile environment—towards financial professionals. The Graham-Dodd Financial Reform Bill basically makes anyone who effects or practices securities transactions or provides investment advice to others to be treated as a fiduciary, or someone who acts exclusively in the best interests of their client. The intention is noble, but will increase the legal and compliance fees associated with extra regulatory requirements, which will translate to higher fees to the client anyway. Firms will increasingly reject smaller investors and only work with the wealthiest clients.

Finally, the markets themselves are victims of an increasingly computerized world. *Institutional Investor* estimates that 50-70% of trading now done in American exchanges is executed by high frequency trading computer program. Because the spoils in program trading go to the ones with the fastest microprocessors and the best algorithms, regulators are already sensing that the average investor is increasingly at the mercy of those who are making one or two cents a trade, a hundred thousand or million times a day, day in and day out. Instead of normal bull or bear moves, the use of leverage among these program traders has implications that act as an amplifier, taking normal up or down moves and magnifying them into major market movements. When these are coupled with the psychology of "get me out now at any cost" that obtained for many in 2008, there can be little doubt that selling low and missing the subsequent recovery will impoverish thousands.

Imagine, for a moment, that you had $1 million at the beginning of 2006. You and a planner put a financial plan together. and didn't update it until now. Your financial plan had an asset allocation section. It read:

1.1.2006

50% domestic (US) stocks ($500,000)
25% international stocks ($250,000)
20% bonds ($100,000)
5% cash ($50,000)

Total: $1,000,000

The plan said to rebalance annually, but for some reason, this part of the plan didn't get enacted. The portfolio was doing well, your planner didn't call, and you saw no need to make an adjustment, because you were making money.

But then what would happen? Well, if this program was begun on 1.1.06, the allocation might look like this on 1.1.07:

1.1.2007

55% domestic stocks ($578,950)
30% international stocks ($315,850)
10% bonds ($104,330)
5% cash ($52,380)

Total: $1,051,510

Now let's go to 2008.

1.1.2008:

54% domestic stocks ($610,734)
31% international stocks ($351,130)
10% bonds ($111,602)
5% cash ($54,863)

Total: $1,128,329

Here we can see right away that the proportion of bonds in the portfolio has been cut in half—from 20% originally to 10%. What happens next? 2008. The year would have ended looking like this:

1.1.2009:

51% domestic stocks ($384,762)
26% international stocks ($200,144)
16% bonds ($117,450)
7% cash ($55,850)

Total: $758,206

The portfolio lost over 32% of its value in this year. But now look what happens! You call the planner up and say you can't stand to be in the market anymore. The new allocation looks like this:

20% domestic stocks ($151,641)
10% international stocks ($75,821)
50% bonds ($379,103)
20% cash ($151,641)

Total: $758,206

This ensured that the recovery in 2009 was almost totally lost to you. And the wound is fatal! Nearly a third poorer, you vow never to invest significantly in the market again.

So how could this have been avoided? Firstly, by rebalancing each year. Do you need evidence? Let's go back to 1.1.2008, but we'll rebalance to the original asset allocation, then see what happens.

1.1.2008:

54% domestic stocks ($610,734)
31% international stocks ($351,130)
10% bonds ($111,602)
5% cash ($54,863)

Total: $1,128,329

New portfolio mix after rebalancing:

1.1.2008:

50% domestic (US) stocks ($564,165)
25% international stocks ($282,082)
20% bonds ($225,666)
5% cash ($56,416)

Total: $1,128,329

Then let's run them through 2008:

1.1.2009:

51% domestic stocks ($355,424)
26% international stocks ($160,787)
16% bonds ($237,491)
7% cash ($57,431)

Total: $811,133

Comparing this to the non-rebalanced portfolio, we get a difference of ($811,133 - $758,206) = $52,927 of additional wealth at the end of the year. Rebalancing not only protects wealth in bad markets, it improves performance in the inevitable recoveries by ensuring more money goes into discounted assets.

In this case, rebalancing your portfolio would have maintained the original equity, bond and cash weightings, not letting the markets distend them to unusual proportions. How could you have done this? By simply calling your advisor and setting a time to review the existing plan and see if any amendments needed to be made. A simple offsetting 5% of portfolio assets in gold or put options during this crisis—a hedge—would have also stemmed fairly significant losses for most investors.

The point of all this? Even perfect plans fail. But a plan written on a cocktail napkin soundly followed is better than a Ph.D. thesis that just collects dust on the shelves. Don't stop at creating the plan. Keep it. Refer to it. Monitor it. Amend it. Most importantly, once you're satisfied with it, follow it! This makes the difference between a disciplined investor and an emotional investor.

To do:

- Book four appointments NOW in your calendar for you to go over your financial plan over the next four calendar quarters. The first will be with your advisor. The next two can be with anyone else that you trust concerning money—a spouse, a parent or sibling, a good friend. The three criteria for this third party are: 1) you trust them; 2) you like them; and 3) they know what they're doing fiscally. Take them to dinner for this "review." Take notes when you're with them and take the advice they give you back to your planner. Get their feedback, and then call your planner after the third meeting to book the fourth meeting. (It will likely be a different date from the one you booked at first.)
- Create your own statement of financial position and cash flow worksheet. These are relatively straightforward documents that illustrate the net worth and discretionary income you have for a

given time period. Use this link: http://www.startbreakingfree. com/232/how-to-understand-and-create-a-personal-financial-statement-each-month-in-5-minutes/

- Ask your advisor for some long-term literature on the markets. One of the best pieces available for investors is Franklin Templeton's *77 Years of Bulls and Bears*, available at https://www.franklintempleton. com/retail/pdf/home/splash_PUB/THEME_XBE.pdf.

The misconception:

I have a plan. I got it online.

The reality:

Computer-generated plans, while able to provide generic "advice" on implementing a specific investment strategy or principle, are still far less "leading edge" than a simple interaction involving another human being that knows how to listen.

The proof:

It's said that up to 90% of communication is nonverbal—gestures, posture, eye movements, leg and arm movements, hand motions, smiles and frowns, the way someone holds their head, etc. There's the classic saying in movies: if the scene is about what the scene is about, you're in trouble. This refers to *subtext*—the hidden or true meaning that someone is conveying and really feels but who isn't using words to express it.

Subtext isn't for computers. Subtext is for people. Yogi Berra once said, lamenting reporters, "they only print what I say, not what I mean." Part of the job of a good financial planner is to listen, both to what the client is saying with his mouth and to what he's saying with his body. Money is an emotional topic; it causes stress, elation, mania, depression, and every other major feeling a person can have. Because of this, the only medium able to understand something as complex as a human being who can feel all these things, is another human being who feels them.

Have you ever had a meeting with a professional in which you realized something amazing? Where you had a revelation of some sort? Where you felt exhilarated, vindicated, free? Maybe a teacher showed you a concept in physics that made you want to become an astronomer, or a skilled doctor fixed an injury, allowing you to play volleyball again. This is what can happen when you meet with a *person*—someone who can discern what you really need (not just what you think or say you need) and who takes the time to get to know you. I have seen this firsthand, and I can't think of how it could happen simply using a spreadsheet. Numbers and math produce logic, but people don't make decisions based on logic. They make decisions based on emotion. Humans deal with emotion.

Computers are undeniably a useful tool; look at romance. As of May 2010, 1 in 6 married couples met online. Those are definitely betting odds! But did those computerized introductions remain so? No; they blossomed into relationships that became *personal*—of a person. So keep the spreadsheets and Monte Carlos, but use a person to help you with your plan as well. They understand emotion—and they still work in power outages.

To do:

- Ask yourself what your philosophy is towards money. What do you want it for? What are your plans for it? Talk this over with someone close to you that you trust.
- Pay attention to the reaction of the other person when you tell them your goals. Look at their body language and facial expressions. If you could translate it into words, what would they be?
- Do this with two other people you trust and compare the results. Then take these results and share them with your financial planner.

The misconception:

There's no way I will ever have enough time and money to pay for my child's college.

The reality:

The rising costs of college are a significant hurdle to overcome, but proper planning and even modest savings programs done early enough can make a huge impact on the education of a loved one.

The proof:

There are really only three things that can happen with respect to a child's education:

- The child pays;
- The child gets a full scholarship;
- Someone other than the child pays.

Scenario 1 is uncommon and usually only occurs if the child has received an inheritance, etc. Scenario 2 occurs when the child has athletic or academic talent and can obtain some or all of the cost of school. Scenario 3, the most common, typically occurs with a combination of need-based and performance-based aid, whether in the form of grants, gifts, or loans, and the parents' contribution and savings on the child's behalf.

The first rule in saving for college is to begin early. One of the greatest services financial planners can render to clients is to encourage their parents and other relatives to open accounts to save for college at the child's birth. In doing this, a modest savings of even $50 a month compounded at 8% becomes over $24,000 by the time the child begins school. If each parent is able to match this, the child can very quickly amass a significant nest egg for his education. Wealthier grandparents and relatives may be able to contribute more, as well as larger amounts—some may be able to give the full $13,000 annual amount not subject to the federal gift tax. Larger gifts given early really magnify the power of compounding—the same $13,000 at the same 8% rate would grow to over $51,000 by the first day of school!

For families truly strapped for cash, there are an abundance of aid programs in the marketplace.

Nonetheless, there are very few families unable to begin by saving at least a nominal amount, say only a few dollars a month automatically deducted from their pay each period. As this money accumulates and the parent doesn't miss it, the amount can be raised. Depending on the degree of discretionary income in the family, this strategy is typically one that can be begun anytime, by any family. If you can't start with $50 a month, try $25. If you can't do $25, do $10. If you can't do $10, do $5! Whatever amount you start with, make sure you don't miss it. $5 done consistently is better than $100 and then quitting after three months.

For families with more disposable income, a formal education savings needs analysis may be warranted. Any good financial planner will be able to conduct one of these for you. The most important factors in the analyses are the assumptions—the rate of return on investments, the cost of school, and the inflation rate. Probably the most important thing here is to use a conservative inflation rate—most planners use 6%. Warning: the numbers can look daunting! A formal analysis for a family that really doesn't have disposable income may make them feel like saving for college is harder than ever. A better approach here is simply to recommend that they start, that they start now, and that they start small but *consistent.*

Finally, for those families that have assets that warrant the analysis, the results can be galvanizing for ambitious parents. It can be extremely rewarding to watch the maternal instinct kick into gear while conducting one of these. "It's going to cost *how* much?" said one woman, when I told her that the first year of undergraduate costs at Harvard would be over $105,000 by the time her newborn niece turned 18. "We have work to do," she said, turning to her husband.

Perhaps this is the most important lesson of all: attitude. Instead of making the common mistake many families make, which is to look at how much they haven't saved, families pursuing this excellent endeavor for their children need to focus on what they have saved and are saving. As Arthur Ashe so eloquently said: "Start where you are, use what you have, do what you can."

To do:

- Whether you have children or not, start a college fund. Begin with an extremely nominal amount—say $10.00 per month. Have it automatically deducted from your checking account, or, better yet, deducted from your pay, possibly into an online savings account. http://www.ehow.com/how_2819_start-college-fund.html
- Set up a second automated transfer to occur every six months from the online savings account into a brokerage account or retirement

account, depending on what your planner recommends for your specific situation. Then have them invest it.

- If you're not missing the money by the third month, double it. If you're still not missing it three months later, double it again. Finally, if after three more months you're still not missing it, double it still again. If you can hold this pattern, at 8% you'll have over $35,000 in 18 years. If each parent saves, that's $70,000.

Misconception:

My credit is unfixable.

Reality:

Credit depends on business character and habit. If character and habit can be mended, credit will follow.

Proof:

Mohammed Yunus won the 2006 Nobel Peace Prize for his work in the field of microfinance. This discipline, like any financial discipline, has more than one application, but one of them best illustrates the concept of credit—the granting of microloans to indigent but industrious and conscientious female entrepreneurs based on personal references rather than a formalized reporting and scoring system. Yunus made his first loan—for 27 dollars—in 1976 to 42 businesswomen in the village of Jobra to make bamboo furniture. He was one of the first to realize that entrepreneurial borrowers would never be able to contribute to the economic well-being of a nation as long as they were discriminated against by usury.

These women typically had to have several positive character references; these were the deciding factor in whether or not they would pay the money back. The ones who received positive references got the money; the others didn't.

The women who got the money had the character. The women who got the money had the habit of dealing fairly with others in business.

Our system has similarities, though the balances are typically larger. 35% of the credit score assigned to individuals in the US is determined by how quickly they pay their bills. If they have a bill 30 days past due, that's a black mark. 60 days past due, another black mark. And so forth. The first rule in improving your credit score is to pay all your bills on time. The rest of the score is divided among how much debt you have and what type it is (30%), how long you've had it (15%), what variety of credit accounts you're using (10%), and how many credit accounts you've opened in the past 6 months (10%). Paying attention to the first two is the simplest way, therefore, to improve 65% of your credit score.

Another easy way to indirectly improve your credit score is to save more. The more assets you have, the easier it is to be able to anticipate emergency bills, save for extra payments on debt, and get rid of more principal more quickly on secured debt.

There's another reason to save more: it creates discipline. It's sometimes difficult for people to consume products and services beyond their reasonable ability to afford them. In other words, subtract your expenses (including your savings!) from your income. The total is how much money you have for the assumed period. If you're having a hard time living within that amount of money, there are two ways to deal with it: the easy way, and the severe way.

The easy way is to simply have a separate account for your current (this cash flow time period) needs and your bills. Don't raid the bill account, and make the money last. The severe way? Give the money to a second person and then have them allot it to you. The difficulty here, of course, is that those who need this method the most are the least likely to ever do it. Nonetheless, having someone give you an allowance can work.

Finally: go over your debts. For many people, simply the act of getting all the statements of obligation (bills) in one place and looking at them can help them to become more active in managing them. By forming the *habit* of always paying debt on time, analyzing the total debt held, and establishing a savings program by treating the savings as another bill, investors form the (financial) *character* that creates good credit.

To do:

- Gather your bills and examine the liability side of your own statement of financial position. Try and categorize them into long-term liabilities (taking longer than one year to pay back) and current liabilities (those due within the next year). Talk the statement over with your significant other, trusted friend or family member, or financial planner.
- Establish an arrangement with your bank for a nominal sum to be automatically deducted from your pay each period to improve your credit. Use the method outlined previously under misconception #5 (college costs).
- Try the receipt test for 30 days. For this period of time, keep every receipt for every single thing you buy and put it into an envelope or bag. Look at it after 30 days time. Share the results with the person you shared the liability side of your statement above with.

Misconception:

Time is money. I don't have any to spare on a plan.

Reality:

Designing and executing any decent financial plan can return ten, a hundred, or even a thousand times as much as the time spent in terms of long-term financial, familial, and emotional stability.

Proof:

The most dramatic example of "return on planning" occurs in risk management—specifically, insurance. The premature death of a primary breadwinner can cause permanent and irreversible financial damage to a family. Yet many busy parents can't find the time to do a needs analysis, preferring to work nonstop. As Hemingway said: Motion is not action! According to figures from Kaplan University, most of the life insurance in force in the United States is term insurance—typically the kind you get from work, often as a multiple of salary. But most of the insurance death benefits collected are on whole life policies. While there are numerous other indicators of the public's attitude towards life insurance, this is perhaps the most telling. In short: people take the path of least resistance when managing for the very real possibility that they may die during the peak of their earning power, leaving their family to deal with the compounded tragedies of a lost loved one and a shattered financial foundation.

Perhaps no other financial product in the world offers such a disproportionate return on the amount invested as life insurance. The probability of a return is one: you will die. As long as the company is solvent and the premiums are paid, the death benefit check will be there when the insured dies. Premiums paid, even on whole life policies, are often very small in proportion to the face amount of the policy. Adding in the income and (possibly) estate tax-free nature of the death benefit when properly structured, the returns can be astronomical. Let's look at a simple term policy.

An employee at a financial firm pays a monthly premium on term insurance. In this case, say it's a 39-year old male in good health who doesn't smoke. He pays $8.06 per pay period (26 times a year) for coverage of $350,241. Compounded at 3% for inflation, how much has he paid in premiums by age 81? $17,624! If he dies and his heir gets the $350,241, that's over an 1,800% return! (Keep in mind I'm not taking inflation into account here.)

What if he dies earlier, say at age 44? In this case, the return soars to over 800,000%! These numbers are somewhat comical, and no one plans to die young. But even a cursory glance at term insurance makes the case for overinsuring, rather than underinsuring, quite attractive.

Other areas where risk management can be critical are:

- Disability insurance, especially for high earners
- Long-term care insurance
- Superannuation insurance (the risk of running out of retirement income, usually addressed with some type of annuity)
- Individual & commercial insurance
- Property & casualty insurance

While these other areas are typically not as disproportionate in their return/ risk ratios as life insurance, they can be an integral part of financial planning for an extremely wide cross-section of clients.

If this much can be avoided with proper risk management, what more could be accomplished with an adequate plan to address all the other facets of a client's life: again, tax, estate, retirement, investments, and overall financial issues? The words of Churchill praising the intrepid airmen of the Second World War come to mind: "Every morn brought forth a noble chance, and every chance brought forth a noble knight." Every chink in a client's financial armor is a "noble chance" for a good financial planner. Take the time to check your chinks!

To do:

- If you feel pressed for time, go to this link: http://www.chetholmes. com/articles/mastering_time_management.htm
- Make creating or checking your financial plan one of your "top six" tasks for the day.
- Make doing something for one of the most critical areas of your plan one of your top six tasks in perpetuity. You'll be astonished at how much things can improve when you focus!

Misconception:

Financial planning is only for the wealthy.

Reality:

Financial planning touches on the lives of almost everyone, from the homeless to billionaires.

The proof:

Many people have the same complaints about financial planning that Charlie Brown has for the dictionary: if you know how to spell the word, you don't need to look it up, and if you don't know how to spell it, you can't find it. In the same way, the rich are already rich, and don't need a planner to help them get richer. Likewise, the poor who are looking for a planner to make them rich will be looking long and hard, particularly if financial markets continue their sideways path.

The truth is that most of us are in between these two extremes—a net worth (less than we'd like, sometimes), and discretionary income (again, not always as much as we want). Not only are these two basic measurements of financial health indicative of the public's appetite for financial planning, but the other focus areas of the discipline are just as important and often overlooked. These are essentially retirement, estate and tax planning, risk management and insurance, employee benefit planning, investment planning, and education planning.

The clients with more modest assets need basic financial planning advice: the establishment of an emergency fund, credit and debt management, cash flow management, and so forth. Those who are nearer to the twilight of their working careers and who have more substantial assets need sound advice on retirement and investment planning. Finally, the wealthiest clients often need the most complex advice of all: tax and estate planning. The federal and state governments' insatiable appetite for tax revenue can necessitate very nimble advisors in these spheres.

And what about the poorest people? Indirectly, the proper management of any individual's resources—rich or poor—allow them to live longer on their own, in many cases delaying dependence on Social Security, Medicare and other entitlements. These delays help to lengthen and strengthen the solvency of these programs, and ensure that they can do what they were meant to do: help the members of society who need them the most. Finally, successful firms, employees and customers often spend a good deal of time volunteering for organizations providing the things that the most vulnerable members of society need: food, lodging, medical care, and education and counseling.

If you're a practicing financial planner reading this, maybe you've run into a situation where you met an individual who you sensed didn't meet your typical client criteria make an arch comment: "I could use you. I need to get rich." Help that individual. It will benefit the rest of the world, even if it doesn't directly benefit you. The greater your knowledge, the greater your responsibility.

To do:

- Take a look at the CFP Board's 2009 National Consumer Survey on Personal Finance. You can find it at www.CFP.net/downloads/ CFP Board 2009 National Consumer Survey.pdf.
- Look at page 8, Core Questions. Examine the issues raised by the respondents. How do these issues correspond to you own?
- If you see areas where your own planner missed when you last met with them, contact them and straighten the issue out for your next meeting. Depending on the urgency of the issue, you may need to schedule another meeting.

Misconception:

Borrow all you can and focus on maximizing assets.

Reality:

Focusing too much on the asset side of the personal balance sheet is just as bad as focusing too much on the liability side. By focusing too heavily on asset returns, clients can have their financial position wrenched out of proportion permanently by increasing debt costs as well as price slides in falling markets.

Proof:

This is likely the least commonly held misconception today, given the depths of the turmoil in the wake of the subprime collapse and its impact on most major world markets in 2008. Global leverage is (wisely) believed by most analysts to be the cause of the meltdown—essentially, the belief that borrowing costs would stay permanently low, and that asset (here, housing) values would remain permanently high. Isn't that all it really boils down to?

The problem is what happens when three forces join hands: poor fundamentals, securitization, and derivatives. The fundamentals of mortgage underwriting in the subprime sector in much of states like Nevada, Florida, and California were poor. Nonetheless, if this isn't commonly known, it doesn't mean that asset prices have to fall—lots of securities with poor fundamentals go higher in price, as long as someone's out there to keep hitting the buy button. But when these securities get packaged, and repackaged, and bedizened with various options and bets on whether or not they'll default and by how much, their impact on world markets doubles, triples, multiplies tenfold. This is because there can be more buyers and sellers buying the same batch of securities and bidding it higher and lower all the time, spiking the volatility to enormous levels.

History rhymes. In 1929-1932, margin ratios allowing investors to buy a dollar stock with a dime magnified the financial ruin felt by thousands from the collapsing prices of financial assets. In 2008, the same basic principle revealed its power in the real estate markets: excess leverage is fine for awhile if the asset only goes up, but devastating when it falls. It can be hard to see the forest at times—there's a lot of attention given to what happened in the last twenty minutes. The problem is that it's still there; you just need to look for it.

To do:

- Evaluate the price cycle of the asset you're thinking about investing in. If it's a home, do a little research about the price rhythms of similar homes in your area. If it's a financial asset, look at charts with various timeframes—daily, weekly, monthly.
- Make sure you clearly understand the terms of the debt you're thinking about taking on. Can the rates change? Can the payments change? How? Do you have a contingency plan in case you need emergency cash?
- Ask the "worst case" questions and take a hard look at what would happen to your debt situation if the asset price fell significantly—maybe as much as 50%. What would happen if it went to zero? Could that happen? There were securities that lost 100% of their value in both the crashes of 2000 and 2008.

Misconception:

Always pay down debt first and focus on minimizing liabilities.

Reality:

Every situation is different. No two investors have the same geographic location, market returns and interest rates, investment time horizons and risk tolerances, age, health and family relationships, employment situations, and general financial position and cash flow.

Proof:

Assets rise and fall in price. This statement is so obvious it's overlooked, yet this is the single reason that every investor who ever lived wasn't successful. When contemplating an investment, ask two questions: 1) What is it really worth? 2) Where does it stand right now in relation to its long, medium, and short-term price cycles?

Suppose you know a couple in their late 60s, Susan and Stan. They have a small emergency fund and live off of Social Security and a modest pension from Jim's former job as a lineman for a power company. They also have a $200,000 brokerage account and still owe $150,000 on their mortgage. Their house is assessed at $250,000. Because the markets have performed poorly in the past few years, Stan and Sue decide to take the money out of the markets and pay down the house. The reasoning: the mortgage debt is at 5.75%, but the markets have lost money three years running.

So far, so good. But now what happens? The house, sitting on the tip of a real estate bubble, plummets in value to $175,000. Some equity is still there and it's all paid for, but Susan and Stan were planning on cashing out at $250,000 and taking the rest to put a downpayment on a second house in another location. That plan won't work now, because they have $100,000 less equity than they did a year ago. Meanwhile, the stock market has rebounded significantly, returning 30%. Susan and Stan are living in a paid for house, and they have no debt. But they ran out of one market that subsequently went up thirty points, and into one that fell forty points. Because they decided to pay off debt at all costs, irrespective of any other data, they've failed to embark on the journey they planned on. It turned out their "safest" asset—their personal residence—was also susceptible to bubbles.

The solution? Run scenarios. Risk management is what needs to be done here. Different planners look at debt management differently, but many clients view all debt as a scourge. It isn't. Debt can be used as a tool to leverage existing assets and take advantage of market trends. The key is having a knowledgeable advisor to help you discern where the major four markets—stocks, bonds, currencies, and commodities—are in their price cycles and making sure you take those considerations into account.

To do:

- Ask your planner to create three scenarios: one in which you pay off minimal consumer and secured debt, one in which you pay it all off in full, and one halfway between. Ask them to walk you through the ups and downs of each strategy.
- Ask your advisor to explain to you where each major asset class is in terms of its price cycle.
- Ask your advisor how they arrived at this conclusion and what it means to your borrowing and liability management strategy.

Misconception:

B UY TERM AND invest the difference.

Reality:

Numerous considerations—such as market fluctuations, insurability, cost, and investment savvy of the party involved—enter into the purchase of life insurance.

Proof:

I knew a lovely couple who were married for 55 years before the husband passed away. He had often offered to include his beloved spouse in the family's finances, but she had always deferred to his judgment. While his judgment was generally sound, she was surprised when after his passing she received a check from the insurance company—for a fifth of what she had been told the policy's face value was! She called the agent, who reluctantly explained to her that her husband had been borrowing from the policy and had depleted most of its value.

"Wait," I hear you saying. "Isn't that an argument *for* term, not against it?" No. It's simply an argument showing that the very features that attract many purchasers to life insurance in the first place can work against them, defeating the purchase of the policy. In sum, every situation is different.

Take term. In 2000, if the cost of a whole life policy was $1,500 a year and the cost of a term policy was $150 a year for the same coverage, would the one buying the term and investing the difference in the S & P 500 be happy? Not likely; he would have $13,358—a loss of 10% on the amount put in over a *decade*. Even a modest growth of 2% in a whole life policy—and some pay 4% or higher—would put the cash value closer to $16,300. This could be borrowed against, used to pay premiums, or simply left to accumulate. Most importantly, it's a real asset that can be counted on the client's balance sheet, unlike the term insurance, which has no cash value.

But what if the term investor was sharp enough to take the difference and just sock it away in gold for the decade? Then his return on buying term and investing the difference would have been a whopping 287%—he nearly tripled his money!

The bottom line is that it's impossible to assign a blanket formula to any investor. Many clients say things like "I hate insurance," "Insurance companies are thieves," and even "I don't want my kids getting anything." But as mentioned before, insurance provides the most disproportionate amount of *predictable* return on money invested of any asset in the financial markets. (I say *predictable* because the leverage available in some markets, like the currency and futures markets, can provide gains of 100:1 or more with the right price movements. But these are extremely volatile and speculative.) And you won't quickly find anyone who's received a sizeable death benefit check and who needed it saying anything bad against it. Finally, insurance can provide incredible income and estate tax savings for the most affluent clients; typically the policies provided here are whole life policies. It seems that the more an investor has to lose, the more they gravitate towards whole life, because of the various tax benefits involved.

To do:

- Have your advisor run a calculation on several term policies and several whole life policies. Ask them to explain the differences, knowing your entire financial situation.
- For the whole life policies, ask them to calculate the cost per thousand of coverage. If they don't have a method of doing this, ask them to use the Belth formula, devised by Professor Joseph

Belth of Indiana University. This link takes you there: <u>http://cdn.</u>
<u>financial-planning.com/forums/viewtopic.php?p=1907971&sid=</u>
<u>1340e376da9ede7f1007d179e50039e2</u>

- Make sure your advisor understands your cash flow, age, health, assets and liabilities, family size, earnings of each spouse, and any other factors you can think of that would impact your decision-making process.

Misconception:

I have enough insurance through work.

Reality:

The simple fact that most insurance death benefit paid is from whole life policies while most policies in force in the country are term points towards the fact that the average American is underinsured.

Proof:

The average 20-something in 1994 was estimated to have eight different jobs throughout his working life. In 2010 the same average 20-something has *already* been through seven jobs. The typical American workplace has vanished for many, relegating life insurance and other employee benefits to the background in a world where financial survival is the key focus of many. Because so many jobs are ephemeral and transitory, the major concern of life insurance—to provide liquidity for loved ones in a tragedy—is outdated for much of the younger population that, paradoxically, is most able to benefit from it because of the low cost.

What about the Baby Boomers, the tens of millions of Americans born between 1946 and 1965 who make up the bulk of individual US retirement assets and entitlement obligations? If the median American wage was $44,389 in 2007 (Source: Wikipedia), then the average American worker might receive 4 times salary, or about $177,500. At a withdrawal rate of 5%, this would only provide for $8,875 per year for a surviving spouse, assuming no debt. If debt exists, that sum will shrink. An even worse scenario would be for the surviving spouse to discover that the decedent spouse's benefits had run out and the life insurance policy had been terminated. In this case, the emotional wreckage caused by the loss of the spouse is compounded by the prospect of insolvency.

The basic problem is that most clients are never made aware of how much insurance they really need. In the case of simple life insurance coverage, there are several phases to consider. The first one is, how much money is needed to pay off any existing long-term debts at death, including mortgages, auto loans, school loans, credit card loans, etc.? The second is a series of calculations that requires a good deal of discipline: how much is needed to provide the same standard of living for the survivors until the youngest child turns 22? How much is needed to pay for college for each child? When the last child leaves and the surviving spouse is alone, how much is needed to provide for her from then until her own retirement? How much is then needed during that retirement? Finally, have estate costs and an adequate emergency fund been included in the analysis? Does the couple wish to add coverage for the unexpected?

Most Americans bringing this short series of questions to their own financial planner will be astonished at the amount of insurance they need—and don't have. In the house of financial services, risk management is the foundation everything is built on. Employee benefits provide excellent supplemental coverage in many cases. But most clients really wanting to ensure that their houses are protected from the storms, winds and rains of life will need to ask if these things should be the only thing their financial felicity is standing on.

To do:

- Ask your planner for a formal life insurance needs analysis.
- Find out what processes your planner has in place to determine coverage for long-term care, disability, and retirement income insurance.
- Look at your death benefit through your policy from work if you have one. Compare it on paper to the debts you would want paid off at your death. How do they compare?

Misconception:

I hate insurance. The agents are like used car salesmen without the elegance.

Reality:

Insurance agents are usually compensated by commission, so their pay system gives them an incentive to sell as much of it as they can. Nonetheless, the work of a skilled insurance agent can greatly assist a client, especially in the areas of determining the appropriate amount and method of coverage, stability of the insurer, and making sure that the policy stays in force.

Proof:

The problem with this misconception is the same as in so many other areas of finance, and in many other business fields as well—reps are encouraged to sell based on corporate initiatives first and client needs second. Nonetheless, many of the reps in the industry are not only good salespeople but good businesspeople. Much of what you need to know about someone can be found online. Google your insurance person, just like a large company would if they were considering you for a position. Going online to a website like LinkedIn can quickly show you someone who is skilled in their field and who has a consistent record of satisfying clients. Call and ask if you can have the names of a few of the prospective rep's clients to call and gauge their feelings.

More importantly than the ability to search for someone's records online is having a method to gauge what he or she knows about the product you're considering. Check your area community college, vocational school or university to see who's teaching classes in finance. Call one of the instructors up and ask for tips on how to find someone who will address what you're looking for, not what will help the rep have a good month.

If all else fails, and you're resolute in going it alone, make sure you're extremely conservative in the assumptions you use for how much insurance to buy. If it's life insurance, try and have a way to calculate how much the policy costs per $1,000 of coverage, possibly using the Belth Method described above. Use three or four good online insurance needs analysis tools—they're out there! You know you're on the right track if they come close to the same amount of coverage.

If you do decide to work with a professional, make sure you ask them these questions:

- What kind of coverage do I need?
- How does it help me?
- How long do I have to read the policy and examine it before I can change my mind? (i.e. what is the free look period?)
- How long does the policy stay in force?
- What happens if the insurance company becomes insolvent?
- How likely is that to happen?
- Do you get paid differently depending on which policy I choose? How?

To do:

- Take a look at the following needs analysis tool online. The site is through LIFE, a nonprofit. http://www.lifehappens.org/life-insurance/life-calculator
- Compare MSN Money's calculator, found here: http://moneycentral.msn.com/investor/calcs/n_life/main.asp
- Finally, look at Cigna's calculator. http://www.cigna.com/our_plans/disability/calculator/lifeneeds_LP.htm

Misconception:

I don't need it. I don't have a big estate.

Reality:

With the exception of those whose age and/or health prevents them from getting it, almost anyone who is insurable at reasonable costs can benefit from additional life insurance.

Proof:

One of the strangest things about people is that they claim to want a sure thing, but often quail when presented with it. One of the best examples of this phenomenon in finance is the prospect of adding life insurance coverage. Many clients of financial planners segregate their advisors: the stockbroker, the insurance person, the banker, etc. Rarely do planners hear clients embrace adding coverage with enthusiasm, especially with healthy clients. Part of this is undeniable: it's never pleasant for most people to contemplate their own death. But let's look at the uses of life insurance proceeds:

- Paying off outstanding debts at death
- Maintaining the same standard of living during the surviving spouse's pre-retirement and retirement periods
- Paying the children's educational costs
- Providing money that can be saved and invested for future generations
- Charitable causes

The last of these is possibly the most overlooked in finance, particularly among clients who may not think of themselves as wealthy. Many claim they can't afford to give more. If they can't afford to give more in life, why not make arrangements at its end for a favorite religious, educational, scientific, or humanitarian group to be the beneficiary of a policy?

The second argument against this misconception is even more obvious. If you had a big estate, the argument goes, you need life insurance to pay estate taxes. This is true. But if you don't have a big estate, the reason is probably at least partially due to the fact that one of your ancestors didn't buy a lot of insurance in the first place! Perhaps one way to break this cycle is to devote additional resources to the one strategy that provides the most certain and substantial "instant estate"—the humble life insurance policy.

To do:

- Really think for a few minutes about a material thing you always wanted but didn't receive until later in life, or perhaps not at all—a boat, an extended cruise, your own business, art lessons with a master. Do a bit of homework and see how much it would cost today.
- Imagine for a moment that you received a bequest of this amount (unless it's ridiculously huge) just when you wanted this thing the most.
- Find out from a planner, online, or a friend in the industry how much it would cost in life insurance premiums to obtain a policy with this face value. If you're uninsurable, use the age and health of the closest insurable person to you.

Misconception:

I don't trust it. The insurers aren't creditworthy.

Reality:

It's relatively easy for any consumer evaluating an insurance policy to examine, with complete transparency and from multiple agencies, the credit rating of the company they're contemplating doing business with.

Proof:

To paraphrase Churchill again: "Democracy is the worst form of government ever practiced by man, except for all the others." The same could be said of the American free market insurance system, even the ratings agencies that determine the credit ratings of its members. To illustrate what goes on behind the determination of a rating on an insurance company, let's turn to the procedures put in place by A.M. Best, the nations' oldest insurance ratings agency. Best, which began to issue credit ratings in 1906, lists fifteen major types of data they use in determining the credit rating of a likely insurer. They are:

- Annual reports—last 5 years' worth
- Audited financial statements of parent and consolidated companies
- Internal and external actuarial reports
- Organization structure, both parent and subsidiaries
- Management structure, board of directors and key executive committees
- Biographical information on principal officers
- Strategic business plans/five-year projections(assumptions)/ownership/capital resources
- Capital management strategies/investor/sponsor strategy
- Competitive advantages/disadvantages
- Completed Best's Supplemental Rating Questionnaire
- Reinsurance contracts
- Catastrophe management strategies (P/C insurers)
- Key distribution partners
- Company's investment guidelines
- Any other information deemed relevant to the rating process

Can you imagine the due diligence going on here? Perhaps you've done work along these lines yourself, volunteering for nonprofit agencies such as the United Way, helping them to determine who can apply for funding and who can't. Typically, for these types of determinations, the basic criteria are a great deal simpler: the basic question is whether the management is competent and honest and the company is solvent. Even for this simple decision, however, financial statements, audit reports, tax forms, meeting minutes, and data generate hundreds of pages per application. Is it thinkable that the audit processes for multimillion and billion dollar companies would be less? From the list above, it appears that would-be insureds can take heart. Not only are the basic financial statements required, but an in-depth analysis of the insurer's competitors, their officers, and even their distribution partners are required. The last is particularly interesting; a company with a sterling record using a less-than-savory business partner will see an effect on their rating.

The second point: consumers don't have to choose just one agency doing all this due diligence. There are four additional major credit ratings agencies in the US that regulate insurance: Standard & Poor's, Fitch, Weiss, and Moody's. A cursory comparison among these separate agencies minimizes credit risk even further. Consumers with the "straight A students only need apply" mentality can have a very easy time with this: one glance at a company's "report card" can tell a customer everything she needs to know before buying. Given similar premiums and coverages, any good financial planner will steer a client towards the company with the highest overall rating among these agencies.

To do:

- Visit A.M. Best's website to get an idea of their credit rating methodology. http://www.ambest.com/ratings/methodology/bcrm.pdf
- Look at the ratings websites of three of the largest insurers: http://www.metlife.com/about/corporate-profile/ratings/index.html
- http://www.newyorklife.com/nyl/v/index.jsp?contentId=8668&vgnextoid=202aa2b3019d2210a2b3019d221024301cacRCRD
- http://www.investor.prudential.com/phoenix.zhtml?c=129695&p=irol-ratings
- If you have an existing insurance policy, ask your planner for information his firm might have on their credit rating.

Misconception:

It's morbid. I don't want my family waiting for me to die.

Reality:

People die, whether family members wait for it or not and whether clients want to talk about it or not. If clients are worried about their families "waiting for them to die," they can buy the insurance in confidentiality.

Proof:

Insurance fraud losses totaled about $80 billion in the US in 2006, according to estimates from the Coalition Against Insurance Fraud. Most of this is property and casualty insurance—estimates for 1996 said that 21% to 36% of auto insurance claims contained elements of suspected fraud. Fortunately, life insurance fraud claims are mercifully lower, but can be downright diabolical compared to these other types of claims. One business executive, for example, collected $600,000 in insurance money after setting fire to his own home—with his ninety-year-old mother trapped in the basement to make it look like a suicide! He was later sentenced to 190 years in federal prison.

Most families, happily, would confess that their family problems are far less serious than this executive's. But many have financially independent children or family members they love but simply don't see eye to eye with. Some may also have twenty-something or even thirty-something dependent children who simply never learned to live on their own. Underinsuring to "punish" these beneficiaries isn't simply uncharitable and unkind, it's financially foolish.

A happy medium exists: choosing a beneficiary who will act in accordance with the client's wishes and know what they would have wanted. There isn't always an easy principle to follow here—sometimes your beneficiaries aren't who you'd expect! One client of mine, a wonderful woman with two older siblings, had one sister who she hadn't spoken with in twenty years. On her sister's deathbed, my client was astonished to receive a call from the attorney-in-fact of her older sister. It was the maintenance man from her apartment building in Florida, who had been taking care of her routine needs for eleven years. He was closer to her than anyone in her own family. Does the probability exist that this man will receive death benefit proceeds from policies on her life? My client is betting on it.

So what's the point? No matter your argument with your family members, no matter how irresponsible they are, even if you have no relationship with them at all—put them on your policies. A wise man said, "We bring nothing into the world, and we can take nothing out of it." If you don't put your family on, put a close friend, someone you trust. Let your death bring more than pain and loss to your loved ones, whoever they are. Let it bring some monetary consolation to those who mourn you the most in that day.

To do:

- Think about who matters the most to you in the world. What would you want them to have if you died today?
- Think about those naturally closest to you, especially those you don't always get along with. Is your conflict or difference of opinion severe enough to warrant disinheriting them, or underinheriting them?
- If you said yes in the second to-do, ask yourself why. Write the answer down, then explain it to your planner.

Misconception:

I don't need long-term care insurance. Let my kids take care of me.

Reality:

Almost two out of three Americans age 65 or over will need long-term care, whether at home, in an assisted living facility, a nursing home, or adult day care.

Proof:

For those aged 55 and over, medical expenses not covered by insurance are the number one financial concern, according to the 2010 Cost of Care Survey, a study published by Genworth Financial out of Richmond, Va. To be sure, this category is a pretty broad umbrella—it covers everything from contact lenses to knee replacements to DNR treatment. Regardless, anyone holding this misconception simply hasn't seen the numbers. According to the summary of findings from the survey, the median hourly rate for homemaker services ("hands-off" care, like running errands) is $18 per hour. In New York State, the average annual cost is $44,616 ($41,184 in the US). For licensed home health aides, the median rate nationally rises to $19 per hour, while the median cost in New York State is $48,620 ($43,472 nationally). These are 88% and 96% of the median annual household income in the US (2007 figures, provided by Wikipedia). Ouch!

What about adult day health care, where someone is provided care in a facility, but not for 24 hours a day? The rate jumps to $60 per hour ($15,600 median annual expense). Here, as with the other major types of care—skilled nursing (semi-private and private room) and assisted living—the numbers themselves are more expensive, although the average annual expense is lower. What is unusual is the inflation rate for these types of care. Over the past five years, the cost of semi-private rooms has increased by 4.6% a year and the cost of private rooms by 4.5% a year. Assisted living facility costs have risen by 6.7% a year. At that rate they're doubling every 10.75 years!

What about the median cost nationwide for other types of care? According to the study, the median US cost of care for a one-bedroom assisted living facility were $38,220. For a semi-private room in a nursing home, this climbs to $67,525; for a private room, it's $75,190! Hopefully less expensive accomodations might be available—like Manhattan's Upper East Side!

"So what? Like I said, my children can support me," I hear you saying. The problem is that many of them are being affected as well—forty percent of the total long-term care provided in the US is provided to those aged 18 to 64. In addition, many clients are reluctant to be a burden on their adult children, many of which are busy with family responsibilities of their own. The best way to ensure you're covered is to address the problem yourself—again, with the lowly insurance policy.

To do:

- Look at Genworth's Cost of Care Survey. http://www.genworth. com/content/etc/medialib/genworth_v2/pdf/ltc_cost_of_care.

Par.14625.File.dat/2010 Cost of Care Survey Full Report. pdf

- Talk to your planner about long-term care insurance, regardless of your age.
- Talk to someone you know who receives some form of long-term care, whether through home care, a health aide, or in a skilled nursing facility. If you can ask them questions about finances freely, do so.

Misconception:

I don't need liability insurance.

Reality:

You don't need liability insurance, as long as nothing bad ever happens to you again for the rest of your life!

Proof:

Liability occurs if three tests are met, according to Mandell S. Winter and Jeffrey Mershon, co-authors of *Insurance and Employee Benefits*. To be able to prove that someone has a liability,

- There has to have been a breach of duty owed to the injured party;
- Actual damage or loss occurred; and
- The proximate cause of the loss or damage was the breach of duty.

Much of our legal system traces from the laws of antiquity. For example, readers of the Hebrew Bible will remember the story of Lot entertaining the heavenly visitors, even being willing to offer his own virgin daughters to the mob outside (Genesis 18). The US legal system extends this ancient principle to modern property owners. Since this is a more common type of liability, let's look at it for a moment.

There are three types of visitors a property owner can have—a trespasser, a licensee, and an invitee. The only duty that a property owner owes the trespasser is to avoid intentionally harming her. A licensee is someone who has a presumed permission to be on the property—the most common is

JOEL T. REDMOND, CFP ®

a salesperson canvassing the area door-to-door (yes, it still happens) or someone invited inside or to another part of the house. Property owners owe this type of visitor not only means to avoid intentional harm, but warnings of known dangers that aren't obvious.

The final type of visitor a property owner can host is an invitee—someone with the express consent of the owner and who has been permitted onto the property for their benefit. Here, property owners must make unsafe areas safe, or warn invitees of their presence.

So: why all this blather? Well, each of these situations may give rise to a situation in which you may be liable for the medical care and other associated expenses arising when harm comes to someone on your property. How? The answer is as limitless as your imagination. I live on a property on a hill with a deeply sloping yard. If a delivery person fell on that wet yard and slipped a disc, I could be liable for the damages. Bricks falling from the roof, breaking glass on a door pane cutting a nerve in someone's hand, an unmarked pit in the yard—anything that could cause someone harm and that isn't obvious qualifies.

Even more stringent are the rules that govern child visitors. This is true primarily because young children are not held responsible for their own carelessness; the extra duty of protecting them from it devolves on the owner. In this case, it doesn't matter whether the children are there with the owner's consent or not—any injury can become fertile ground for suit.

The good news is that most of these areas are covered in a typical homeowner's insurance policy, specifically under Coverages E and F of Section II. These coverages typically address up to $100,000 of covered legal liabilities of the insured due to unintentional property damage or bodily injury. They also typically cover up to $1,000 of medical costs due to an accident on the premises and can be paid regardless of liability (i.e. even if it was the injured person's fault).

For those who don't need homeowner's or auto insurance, some may choose a comprehensive personal liability policy. This is mainly for occupations in which significant potential for personal liability can arise—law, medicine, and finance preeminent among them. A botched operation, an illiquid and poorly communicated investment or bad trade, or an improperly argued legal brief can open these professionals up to a suit that could not only incur heavy loss, but the total removal of earning power by the loss of a professional license. CPL can compensate for some of this. If an ounce of prevention is better than a pound of cure, perhaps salespeople would have an easier time marketing these types of policies to a devil-may-care world.

To do:

- Ask your planner for an analysis of your own liability coverage, including an analysis of your existing policies. What's covered? What's not?
- Find your homeowner's policy or, if you don't own a home, your auto policy. What are the various coverages? Can you make sense of them?
- Ask your planner if you should consider different coverages. Make sure they explain why.

Misconception:

The best health insurance plan is the cheapest out-of-pocket.

Reality:

Which health care plan to choose depends on the anticipated (and unanticipated) care needed—and the pocket! As with most other aspects of financial planning, the only safe principle to operate by is that the individual's circumstances ultimately dictate the best choice.

Proof:

The best example of health care options is Medicare—the government's four-part health care system for those who are at or near retirement age. The program is an enormous part of the federal budget; it is financed both by a 2.90% payroll tax (employees and employers each pay half) and routine premiums, deductibles, and coinsurance payments that patients provide—some regardless of care, some only as care is provided.

Medicare covers four basic areas of health care: hospital (Part A), medical (Part B), managed care (Part C), and prescription drugs (Part

D). Patients pay for Part A through the above-mentioned payroll tax; there are no additional premiums. Benefits included here are part of the costs of hospitalization, limited skilled nursing home care, and hospice care.

Part B covers doctors' fees and most hospital outpatient services, as well as some related services. This is financed through three separate parts. The first is a monthly Part B premium that starts at $110.50 (in 2010) and increases with the patient's annual income. For example, an individual making $300,000 per year would pay $353.60—the highest premium. This is deducted from the patient's monthly Social Security benefit. The rest of Part B comes from an annual deductible of $155 towards the cost of any covered care for the year, as well as 20% coinsurance for covered expenses. These services include a good deal of non-routine medical care, including home health services, major organ transplants, kidney dialysis, and MRI and CT scans.

Part C essentially provides augmented services to the basic Medicare Parts A & B. This part, called Medicare Advantage, sometimes provides coverage for additional items or extra covered days in the hospital. Some also allow for foreign travel. These extra services often have an additional monthly premium. But the basic difference between the MA plan and the original Medicare is in the way the care is offered—either through a managed care plan or a private fee-for-service plan. In the former, a group of directly Medicare-paid doctors, hospitals, and other providers form a group where patients can go for care; in the latter, private health insurance companies receive the payments from Medicare on a per-capita basis for those receiving care.

Finally, Part D offers prescription drug coverage. There are exceptions, but the general trend in 2010 goes like this: you pay a $30 monthly premium, and then the first $310 as a deductible. Then you pay 25% of the next $2.520, all of the next $3,610 (this is called the "doughnut hole,") and then 5% of anything above $6,440 for the year.

If you're ready to rip this up and throw it away because of all the minutiae, what does that tell you? The plans are complicated, because the human body is complicated. There are numerous points to make decisions on. Here are a few of them:

- Choosing the original Part A/B or Medicare Advantage (Part C)
- Choosing whether or not to use lifetime hospital reserve days under Part A after a 90-day stay, or just pay out-of-pocket
- Choosing whether to buy a Medigap policy to cover some of the non-covered areas under Parts A-D of the original Medicare program
- Whether to use a point-of-service option in a managed care plan under Part C, allowing you to see out-of-network doctors
- Whether and when to apply for Part D, depending on your existing arrangements (keep in mind applying late may raise premiums)
- Which are the doctors and hospitals you trust the most—this may weigh heavily in your decision-making process

The point here isn't to overwhelm you with data. The government has done a superb job of this already—just go down to the Medicare office to your area and talk to someone! The point is that health care is one of the largest, most complicated, and most critical arenas of financial planning for the 76+ millions of Baby Boomers who are currently entering into it, as well as the millions a generation ahead of them who are already in the system. If you could only pick one area of your financial life to use a skilled professional in, choose this one.

To do:

- Visit the Medicare website at www.medicare.gov and check the various options available to you. This site contains comparative data on the Medicare Parts A-D plans, nursing homes, home health agencies, and other vital agencies in your area.
- Arrange a conference call between your planner and Medicare. (You may have to give Medicare permission to speak to your planner on the phone.) The number is 800.633.4227.
- Look at www.medicare.gov/contacts for information on the State Health Insurance Program (SHIP), designed to help you choose an appropriate Medigap policy or long-term care policy.

Misconception:

Insurance is just a way for huge companies to get rich.

Reality:

Insurance is the cheapest and surest way to create substantial liquidity for successive generations.

Proof:

This argument could be leveled against any company—from Apple and GE down to the florist's shop on the street corner selling health & disability insurance on the side. But it's no crime to make money. This is the fundamental goal of capitalism—it's defined as an economic system in which the factors of production are privately owned to make a profit. Contrast this with communism, which is an economic, political, and social system in which the factors of production are publicly owned by and for the state.

The traditional seesaw going on in politics seems to be relatively simple: the ones who are actually making a profit lean towards capitalism, and the ones who aren't lean towards communism. There are always exceptions—sometimes people make so much in profits that they can then turn and devote their lives to criticizing the free market system that allowed them to earn them!

If insurance allows companies to get rich, it allows individuals to get rich as well. Again, no other financial product allows people of very modest means to eventually ensure that their families will have substantial sums of cash in the event of their demise. There was a saying among some stockbrokers in the Thirties—some of the larger customers were "hundred share" men, and the smaller ones were "ten share" men. Insurance allows any "ten share" customer to become a "hundred share" customer—without significant outlay of cash, quietly, steadily.

Possibly the image of enormous skyscrapers with flurries of gold-cufflinked, fast-talking money counters bathing in bills has become the predominant one for the insurance industry. It isn't accurate. Firms don't just write policy after policy without breaking out the magnifying lens. Diligent statistical research has to be done from an actuarial standpoint—not just for profitability but for solvency. Medical due diligence and other controls have to be diligently followed. Competitors ensure that inefficiencies in pricing in any market don't last for very long. And then there's paying the staff, overhead, licensing, commissions, compliance, and the reps who sell.

Insurance isn't a way for companies to get rich, but it is a way for *people* to get rich—in some cases the officers of the company, sometimes the salespeople, but always the customer, if they simply continue to pay the premiums and keep the policy in effect. "What are you talking about?" I hear some of you saying. "You're dead! How are you rich?" Insurance always makes the customer rich—in creating a legacy that can last for generations and into perpetuity.

To do:

- If you own life insurance, compare your current net worth with the face value of the policies you own. Write them down.
- If the face values are more than your net worth, take heart. You actually may have an amount approaching your real need.
- If the face values are less, find out how much it would cost in premiums for you to make the sums match; i.e. to double your net worth at death. Then compare what you would pay (over your life expectancy) to that company to what your heirs would receive.

INVESTMENT PLANNING

Misconception:

F IRE YOUR BROKER when she lags the benchmark.

Reality:

It's impossible for any manager in the world to perpetually beat the benchmark.

Proof:

This hopefully is so obvious that no explanation is needed; but, due to the preponderance of unusual expectations fueled by an ADD-raddled media, one is herein offered.

The oft-quoted statistic is that there are 25% of funds at any given time that aren't able to outperform the S& P 500. To answer this question, let's look at the supposed 25% who have. If I go to the mutual fund screener on Zacks.com, and then I calculate the average annual return of the S & P 500 for the past 1, 3, 5, and 10 years, I find they are 7.42%, -9.10%, -2.54%, and -2.67%. This is without dividends reinvested. (By the way, your numbers will be different by the time you try this than mine were.)

OK. Now let's look at the number of mutual funds period. We get 13,711 no-load funds and 6,405 loaded funds, so our total universe here is 20,116. Entering in the total number of mutual funds that have beat the 1 year .SPX performance, we get 15,382. This is 76.47% of the total amount of funds.

Now let's go to 1 and 3 year performers. This reduces the number of funds to 11,324, or 56.29% of the total funds out there. When we add 5 year numbers into the mix, we get 8,571, or 42.61%. Finally, adding the ten-year number into the mix, we get 4,855, or 24.14%.

OK, pretty good. But now what happens when we add the year-to-date performance in? For the .SPX, it was -3.63%. It doesn't sound like much, but let's add it in and see what we get. This brings it down a little bit more, to 4755 from 4855. So the final number is 23.64% of mutual fund managers that consistently outperformed the Standard & Poor's 500 for every major time period for the past ten years.

But what kind of funds are they? Here's the breakdown:

• Aggressive growth—42
• Asset allocation—145
• Balanced—276
• Convertible securities—32
• Corporate high-yield bonds—228
• Corporate investment grade bonds—299
• Diversified bonds—181
• Energy/natural resources—7
• European—9
• Financials—11
• Flexible—42
• Foreign—216
• Global—128
• Government—96
• Government (mortgage)—86
• Growth—828
• Growth & income—416
• Health care—11
• Income—91

• International bond—98
• Municipal (CA)—97
• Municipal (NY)—80
• Municipal (national)—270
• Municipal (state)—354
• Other—38
• Pacific—32
• Precious metals—38
• Real estate—80
• Small company—477
• Technology—21
• Utilities—28

Of all the fund mixes here, the one used most often as a default setting for many buy-and-hold clients is the asset allocation funds. Typically these will invest in diversified portfolios of stocks, bonds, cash, and sometimes real assets, hoping to outperform the market. But here, only 145 of them outperformed the market—only 3%!

So what's the upshot of all this? The upshot is that, if only 23% of money managers in the industry can consistently beat the index, and only 3% of the ones that do are asset allocation funds, it's unreasonable to expect consistent stellar performance without sector risk, and more unreasonable to change managers based solely on past records. Investment policy and a well-thought out manager selection process, not a performance derby, are the most important things to consider for a consistent return.

To do:

- Examine the various indices on Bloomberg. Which of them correspond to your own investments the most? http://www. bloomberg.com/markets/
- Look at the mutual fund screener on Bloomberg's page. What types of funds have the greatest gains over the past few time periods? http://www.bloomberg.com/markets/mutual-funds/top-funds/us/

- Compare the US fund numbers with the others listed—the UK, Brazil, Germany, Japan, and Australia. How significant are the disparities? Is this attributable to the manager, or are similar gains appearing in all the top funds in that region?

Misconception:

A diversified portfolio of no-loads is enough; I'll be OK with that. Fees are for fools.

Reality:

The general performance of no-load vs. loaded fees is dramatically different, at least according to the above-mentioned screener on Zacks. Of the no-load funds, 2,741 of the total 13,711 beat the S & P 500 over every major time period—a sum of 19.99%. For the loaded funds, we have 2,014 of the total 6,405 profiled, or 31.44%. Basically, choosing a no-load gives you a two in ten chance of outperforming the market, while choosing a loaded fund gives you a three in ten chance. (Again, your numbers may be different, depending on the day you try this exercise.)

This should seem intuitive. If most of the no-load funds are index funds, that's what they're there for—they're there to match the index (minus expenses), not beat it. The point of a sales load and higher expenses should be for increased investment talent and higher long-term returns. This isn't always the case—beating the market consistently is notoriously hard for managers, especially as their capital base grows—but at least the probabilities are more in an investor's favor with a loaded fund. It seems that there is, at least, one justification for investment fees.

"So what?" I hear you saying. "It's not enough to justify switching." Well, rather than look at the simple probability that you'll outperform, let's look at another area often overlooked with respect to fees—tax deductions. According to the US tax code, a miscellaneous deduction exists for any expense for the production of investment income, within limits. When we're talking about mutual funds, separate accounts, investment advisory fees, and so on, we have two limits on the amount you can deduct—first, you're allowed a deduction only to the extent of your net investment income, or the income of the funds minus the expenses. For high-yielding funds, this can be a decent sum. Secondly, you're limited to the amount over 2% of your MAGI—your modified adjusted gross income, which you or your tax professional can help you with. The point? The higher the fee, the higher the deduction.

But the most important aspect of paying a fee is the advisor. When finance is likened to medicine or law as a profession, the more experienced and talented the advisor, the more likely the fee is well worth it. (And this fee is typically itself a deduction, within the limits above.) A good advisor can prevent disasters, such as selling at market bottoms and buying at market tops, educate clients on the history and behavior of the markets, provide fundamental and technical commentary and perspective, and, most importantly, manage risk.

This last is critical, especially when it comes to understanding what "risk" really is. Many clients still have no idea that purchasing power risk is very likely a deadlier foe to them than principal risk. The increased longevity of most clients, combined with rapid rises in health care and other major expenses, makes it almost axiomatic that equities will make up a sizeable component of their investment portfolio. Other risks exist—market risk is still very real—but the real risk of running out of retirement money has the most dramatic impact on an investor taking distributions from his or her retirement plan.

This doesn't mean no-loads aren't useful. They still provide the best way for an investor of limited means to obtain a stake in the markets. But even on Wall Street, you generally get what you pay for—in performance, in tax breaks, and, most importantly, in a professional relationship.

To do:

- Look at a chart of .SPX on StockCharts.com. Look at several periods, for daily, weekly, and monthly numbers.
- Add VFINX onto the same chart. This is the symbol for Vanguard's S& P 500 index fund, the largest no-load in the world.
- Now, entering one of the loaded funds that outperformed the S & P over the time periods found on Zacks mutual fund screener above, plot one of them. If you don't feel like looking, here are a few symbols for you: AABCX, CCGAX, DEVLX, DFBAX, ETRAX. How do they compare?

Misconception:

All the market data is garbage; they only use backward-looking data.

Reality:

With an understanding of context and accounting for inevitable uncertainties, a historical perspective on financial markets is indispensable to successful investing.

Proof:

Many of the simplest indicators of a primary trend in financial markets use historical data. One of the best such illustrations is a simple view of the behavior of the Dow Jones Industrial and Transportation Averages over time. In the classic *Technical Analysis of Stock Trends*, the basics of Dow Theory are laid out, which liken the fluctuations in markets to three aspects of the same thing—the ripples, the waves, and the tide. The ripples are the day-to-day and moment-to-moment fluctuations of traders and speculators; these are likened to the Brownian motion of ripples in the water. You can't predict these.

The waves are larger, medium-term movements in the markets—perhaps one to three months. These have some predictability, but can switch abruptly and are difficult to make major investment decisions on. What long-term investors would be best served by analyzing, the theory says, is the *tide*—the major changes in market direction that you can set your watch by.

How do you measure this? Well, you can go to the trouble of subscribing to services that provide signals of "turns in the tide" for you. There is evidence that such signals are useful. One of the greatest pieces of it is a long-term analysis of the Dow Jones Industrial Average, from 1897 through 2005. According to the authors, a buy-and-hold approach to this average for the time period (108 years—whew!) would have turned $100 into $13,000—a 13,000% return. In contrast, the authors reveal, selling the stocks in the average at "high" tide and then buying in again when "low" tide returns, the $100 turned into $345,000 over the same period, for a 345,000% return! Taking it one step further, what if the stocks in the average were sold short at the "high" signals? This brings the return to $1.9 million—a 1,900,000% return. Clearly, if this analysis proved even half true, a look back assuredly helps investors see further forward.

To do:

- Take a look at the historical averages of .INDU and .TRAN. Chart them against each other. Do you see any patterns?
- Look through the last few bear markets—specifically, April 2000—October 2002 and October 2008—October 2009. What do you see?
- If you're interested in Dow Theory further, examine the performance of the Colby algorithm. This formula, designed by Robert W. Colby of the Market Technicians' Association, is designed to imitate the long-term performance of Dow Theory. Simply put, the formula says: 1. Buy .INDU when .INDU reaches a new 9-trading day high and .TRAN reaches a new 39-day high. 2. Sell/short .INDU when .INDU reaches a new 22-day low and .TRAN reaches a new 166-day low. 3. Cover the short when .INDU reaches a new 36-day high and .TRAN reaches a new 32-day high. 4. Repeat. www.robertwcolby.com

Misconception:

Just buy low P/E stocks and rebalance annually.

Reality:

Low P/E scanning, while one component of a judicious investment policy, should never be the sole factor in making investment decisions. Shorter-term investments magnify this rule.

Proof:

Tweedy, Browne conducted a study of the stocks on the American and New York Exchanges from 1966 through 1990. They determined that a simple purchase of the bottom decile stocks in terms of P/E on each exchange, rebalanced annually, would result in an average annual return of 18% for this period. Well, that's it, right? Case closed.

There are problems with this approach. In the first place, this represented a lot of stock trades, especially towards the end of the period when the number of stocks on these exchanges would have been over 3,000. Thus 300+ individual positions would have to be monitored and possibly traded every December 31. That's a lot of watching, monitoring, and analyzing in a time before every stock quote was on computer in real time for the average investor. Most of all, it's a lot of commissions—especially in a time before discount brokerages had the ubiquity they command today.

Price/earnings ratios are useful; they can be a good measure of how expensive or cheap a stock really is. Essentially if we're saying that a given stock has a P/E of 5, that means that if the earnings per share continue at their current pace, it will take you 5 years of those earnings before you receive your money back (not accounting for inflation). Conversely, you'll receive one-fifth of the price you paid, or 20% of your investment, over the next twelve months, again provided the stock continues its earnings rate. We call this the *earnings yield*.

So why can't we use this as the sole yardstick for investment? There are two main reasons. First, and most importantly, it's possible to buy a low P/E stock at a market or sector peak, or even at the top of that stock's 52-week price cycle. For example, Goldman Sachs (NYSE: GS) was trading at $239.20 at the close on 9 October 2007. This was the day the Dow Jones Industrial Average reached its all-time high of 14,159.65. Even if you reasoned that Goldman was trading at a reasonable earnings multiple—maybe it was ten or eleven times earnings at that point—you would have watched that position tumble over 62% over the next year. And you would have sworn off low P/E "investing" forever.

And you would have been wrong! If you had waited instead to scan the P/Es in November 2008, you would have seen GS get to $53.31 during the week of 11.21. At this point, near-end earnings per share estimates were about $19, so the P/E here looked ridiculously low—this white-shoe firm, the envy of Wall Street, was trading at just over three times earnings! This time, the bet paid off big, if you backed up the truck and shoveled in the shares. By the week of 11.6.09, GS was trading at $171.78—you'd have gotten a 222% return in a single year on an S & P 500 stock.

The second reason low P/E can't be the sole criteria for investment is business fundamentals—if they're deteriorating, there might not be any earnings next year. If you're not willing to crunch the numbers yourself, roll up your sleeves, and look at things like current ratios, quick ratios, debt to asset ratios, and so forth, have your planner do it for you. Better yet, look to the securities research industry, which invests over $1 billion a year in fundamental analysis. A simple way to gauge the consensus of Wall Street research firms is found in Zacks Investment Research's ABR—Average Broker Rating—on a stock. This number takes all of the available analysts covering a stock and groups them into an average. Look at the number of analysts covering the stock, and see what the consensus is—1 is a strong buy and 5 is a strong sell.

To do:

- Go to Zacks Investment Research and go to the stock screening page. Enter a criteria for low P/Es—it might be 5, 4, 8, or a different number, depending on where the market is. How many names do you get? http://www.zacks.com/screening_2/custom/
- Pick a stock position and enter it in. Look up its ABR (Average Broker Rating). See how many analysts cover the stock. Would you still buy it based on its P/E?
- Look at the stock on your charts on stockcharts.com. Where is it in relation to its price cycle?

Misconception:

I watch Bloomberg and read the financial press.

Reality:

News coverage, by its very nature, is backward-looking and is at best a co-incident or lagging indicator.

Proof:

The markets are intelligent because people are intelligent. The largest block trades—those conducted by institutions and between very large fund managers—are typically in anticipation of trends coming in securities markets, not because of past events.

Although it's easy to point out cases in which members of the working press have been manipulated by those who wish a certain outcome, it may be intuitively easier to just imagine what you would do if you wanted that outcome. For example, you have an enormous position in a specific stock, and have made a tidy profit. You don't want to unwind all of it at once, but would like to begin the distribution stage. What could you do? Well, you could make an appearance on a TV show and mention positive attributes of that stock. If you're successful, you might be able to sell at a very healthy profit from your entry. Is this ethical? Well, not exactly. But the object of investing is to make money, right?

Perhaps nowhere in all the world is there such an abundance of data as there are in financial markets, especially the US markets. The 200+ years of figures have been examined, reexamined, wrenched, crunched, finessed, presented, obscured, massaged, and generally done to death. Yet, as we examine them, we find that there is always a new angle, a new sound bite, a new factoid to process and consider. In this age of information, perhaps the direction most investors need to take is to consider which information to reject, rather than which information to keep. Probably 90% or more of it is useless.

Technical analysis is very valuable for this. Rather than digesting earnings reports and statements of additional information, or even world interest rates and the Dow-to-gold ratio, a strong performance case can be made for simply making a habit of buying assets at their 52-week lows. It won't be perfect, but it's simple, and requires a low-information diet. You don't even have to read the Wall Street Journal—just decide which asset class divisions you'll use, figure out how you'll divide the money up, and wait for the right price. Then buy and hold.

For those who are news junkies, there are useful facts the press can dig up. They're smart people, and they're motivated to provide quality coverage. Before digesting the content, though, ask yourself if their goal for providing the story peacefully coexists with your own goal for making the investment. This happens more rarely than you might think, especially if you're a long-term investor.

To do:

- Choose the major asset classes you want to divide your portfolio into. These will likely be stocks, bonds, commodities and currencies.
- Look at the various sectors and divisions of these asset classes by examining ETFs that are intended to imitate their indices. If you simply enter "ETFs" into Google, you'll arrive at a link from iShares, one of the largest providers of ETFs.
- Take a little time and examine which of the various asset classes—in terms of these ETFs—are nearest to their 52-week lows.

Misconception:

I use stop-loss orders.

Reality:

Stop-loss orders can still work for the most liquid publicly traded stocks, but grow more and more dangerous as the markets become more and more dependent on computerized trading.

Proof:

Traders love stop-loss orders. One of their favorite tactics is to determine the order flow of stock trading on the floors and gap a position down to where they can buy below market (at the stop), then place enough buy orders above it to make an immediate profit. The result? Your plan to sell out at 2% below your entry point is immediately triggered, and you lose 2% immediately on your trades.

Have you ever made a trade in a certain position and had it turn against you immediately? Those who look at these situations sensitively will feel as though there's someone on the other side of the computer whose personal mission is to make sure your trade loses money.

There is. Business is business. When you make a short-term securities trade to make a profit, you have competition. There's only so much supply and there's only so much demand for any given security. If the aggregate demand outweighs the aggregate supply, the price will go up. If the opposite is true, the price will go down. That's economics. So how can traders make money on your order? By determining the flow of orders so that the appearance of a series of trades in the short-term gives the opposite impression of movement from what you're anticipating.

Just as there are only two types of players in financial markets—investors and traders—there are two different types of traders. The first type of trader likes to make larger profits over longer periods—he looks for home runs. John Paulson is this type of trader—his legendary bet against the subprime mortgage industry resulted in over $15 billion in profits for his hedge fund and $5 billion in profits for him personally in 2007-2009. The second type is the trader who looks for short-term and high-probability profits—they want to make the spread on each trade, or the difference between the highest bid (buy) price and the lowest ask (sell) price. This type of trader is the one who's on the other side of your computer screen when you place a stop-loss order.

Taking an average trading volume of 20MM shares a day and an average spread of one cent on each stock trade, the average market maker dealing in a specific stock can make $200,000 in one day just on the spreads. And that's if they stay at one cent—which they don't! Goldman Sachs, Merrill Lynch, J. P. Morgan, and Deutsche Bank have typically been the ones making these kinds of trades. Since their traders are typically compensated on how much money they make the firm, it's naïve to think you're going to beat them if you're not practicing full-time. You're not.

Computerized trading is one other arena where stops can automatically hit. Know that any market maker can see your stop orders and very likely has computer programs actively looking for buy and sell stop orders from retail or even other institutional investors. The traders typically aren't sitting watching the screens while they do this; the algorithms (preset formulas) are entered into computers automatically and orders are entered within microseconds of the stop price being reached. Some estimates today say 60% of trading on the exchanges in the US is done by computer program. The end result for the retail investor using stops, at least in the short-term, is that the stops are hit and the trader makes a habit of collecting small losses. If the investor sets the stop wider, those losses can mount.

The worst situation for stop orders is for volatile issues in less liquid markets. Since a stop-loss order is typically a market order that hits when the stop price is reached, falling markets with no bid prices (offers to buy the stock) can result in a very wide spread between the investor's entry and exit prices. In technology issues in the 2000-2002 market, for example, the losses sometimes reached 30%, 50%, or 90% of the position's value.

There are alternatives to stops. For large positions in stocks, a protective collar might be a better solution. A protective or cashless collar is a hedging strategy where calls (options to buy the stock) are sold to other investors above the stock's market price, and then puts (options to sell the stock) are bought with the money collected from the calls. The real gems in most collars are the put options, which allow the investor the right to sell the shares of stock at a preset price for a preset period of time. Typically this strategy is used for corporate executives with large portions of their net worth in one stock.

Maybe the best solution to stop-loss orders is making sure you're buying at the right price. Buying almost any position in March 2009 would have resulted in a nice 12-month gain. Since end-of-the-world scenarios in the market don't come around every year, though, a simple solution is to look and see how close a position is to its 52-week low. You can't do this by itself, of course, but you'd be surprised how often making the proper entry to a stock results in the exit taking care of itself.

To do:

- Ask your planner about a protective collar on a stock you've been purchasing. Ask what price you'd be able to sell at once you got in on the down side, and what price you might lose the stock to another buyer on the up side.
- Go to stockcharts.com and look at the various charts available for free. Examine the same stock you're interested in and see where it is in relation to its 52-week high and low.
- If the stock is reasonably close to the 52-week low (a rare occurrence, admittedly), calculate percentage wise by how much. Watch the stock over a period of time, waiting for the appropriate time to buy. Ask your planner to watch it as well and notify you when it falls to your price.

Misconception:

This stock *has* to go up, because (insert fundamental/business reason here).

Reality:

Securities exchanges are not non-profit agencies. The professionals in their employ are in business to make a profit. This is done by precipitating bear markets as buying opportunities for themselves (buying low) and bull markets as selling opportunities for themselves (selling high). Since many of them trade the markets every day for a living, they don't have the time for the fundamentals to raise the price. They want a short-term profit.

Proof:

Listen to a financial journalist describe a public company. The number one measuring stick for this is the *market capitalization* of the company—the number of shares it has outstanding times the current market price of the stock. This is what the company is worth at any given time as a going concern. In other words, if the board of directors decided the company were to be sold, the market cap is what they could reasonably expect as the sell price.

Not the free cash flow, not the earnings yield, not the intangible assets, not the accounts receivable. Not the goodwill or trademark potential of the company. Not the leadership, or even the customers.

The sell price is based on the *market cap*—the price the stock is going for currently, times the number of shares. This is sometimes counterintuitive, and for those skilled in business valuation, it can create tremendous disparities—which can mean opportunities.

For example: the classic definition of the intrinsic value of a company is defined as the present value of its future cash flows. The easiest way to figure this out is to do it on preferred stock. Typically, this type of stock has no stated maturity, so it continues perpetually, and the interest rate is often high—we'll say it's 8%. To figure out what the intrinsic value of the stock is, we divide the annual dividend by the required rate of return of the investor, as a decimal.

Say the stock has a par value (the value at its first offering) of $25. That means the dividend is $2, or 8% of $25. This is paid annually. To find the intrinsic value of the stock, let's assume we have two investors—one who needs a 7% rate of return and another who needs a 12% rate of return. For the first investor, we get an intrinsic value of $28.57 for the stock ($2 divided by.07). For the second investor, the stock is only worth $16.67—the same $2 divided by .12. Therefore, if the stock is trading in the market at $25, it is 12.5% *undervalued* to the first investor—the market price of $25 is 12.5% less than the intrinsic value of $28.57. To the second, the stock is *overvalued* by a whopping 50%—it's trading for 50% more than its intrinsic value! This investor not only won't buy the stock, he might sell it short.

What's interesting is that the same stock can create a buying opportunity for one, and a selling opportunity for another. This is part of the reason that our securities markets are so liquid—the investors have so many different personalities. (The same principles are used in real estate investing, incidentally; just substitute the net operating income from rents for the dividend, and the capitalization rate for the rate of return.)

So what's the use of all this? Well, if you're spending all your time looking at these cash flows and you know what rate of return you want, you're investing *fundamentally*—for a long-term return based on the financial statements and actual operations and prospects of the business. Fundamental investors look at the business behind the stock.

Traders typically look at one thing—the price behavior of a stock due to supply and demand (order flow). This typically has no relation whatever to the fundamentals on a stock. Why? Think about it. How much do the fundamentals of a company—its net income, shareholder's equity, free cash flows, tangible assets, accounts receivable, etc.—really change over one trading day—six and a half hours, if we're talking about the NYSE? For most companies, the change isn't very much.

But take that same company's common stock, and the price can change dramatically in a single day. In fact, the same business can continue its path through a calendar quarter with unchanged fundamentals, yet the markets can value it at a hundred different prices—from significant discounts to a value supported by those statements to premiums well over it.

Finally, these over and under valuations aren't bound by investor expectations or desires. Companies with fantastic fundamentals can take years to rise to value. Companies with lousy ones can soar in stock price. Simply put, this is because of the forces of supply and demand—the less there is of something, the higher its price, and the contrary.

To do:

- Look at your favorite stock over the past decade on the charts on stockcharts.com. What has its price path been throughout the 2000-2010 market?
- Look up your company's statement of cash flows and financial position on www.sec.gov at the EDGAR website. Check it by year.
- How has the price action compared with changes in the financial position and cash flows?

Misconception:

I can time the market.

Reality:

Although the possibility exists for an individual investor to time the market, the probability of it happening—and happening consistently—is quite low.

Proof:

There are very few places other today where it is so easy to create and destroy massive sums of wealth as in the financial markets. World currency trades amount to $4 trillion US a day. Billions of shares are traded on the NYSE alone. Dow Jones Industrial Average stocks trade tens and even hundreds of millions of shares every day.

These trades represent individuals—people who went to school and studied, many with advanced degrees in economics, math, finance, and other disciplines. Some are merely good businesspeople, some are consummate salespeople. Some are extremely ethical and some are liars. Some will cheat.

Many are extremely adept at using advanced technology and engineering applications to trade like Val Kilmer's character in *Top Gun*—ice cold, no mistakes. Many of them are making millions; more than a few are making billions.

All of them are competing—competing against you and others to try and make money for themselves and their organizations. When you say, "I can time the market," what does that mean? It means you can outperform, on a consistent basis, the millions of others throughout the country and the world who are trying to do exactly the same thing, at the same time.

You can do that, can't you? Sure you can. You can also become Deputy Director of Finance for the World Bank, run a mile in under 3:50, or win next year's Academy Award for Best Original Screenplay.

Do you think you will, though?

Jonathan Knee, author of *The Accidental Investment Banker*, noted that one of the techniques managers used at Goldman Sachs was to tell 80% of the staff that they were in the top 20% of the organization. "I am *not* fifth quintile!" was the common sniff heard when the quality of someone's work was brought into question.

Four people out of five aren't in the top 20% of anything. One is. The same rule applies to the securities markets. Kaplan University figures reveal that as of 2007, 75% of fund managers were unable to consistently outperform the S & P 500. Fund managers typically have advanced degrees in finance, tweedy and rather thick designations like the CFA or CIMA, and often all of the energy and optimism of youth. The difficulty is that, to consistently outperform the market, you have to be able to make decisions ahead of the curve and keep making decisions ahead of the curve. Intuitively, this is quite difficult, largely because success leads to pride, which leads to indolence and sloppiness, which inevitably leads to underperformance.

Is this an argument for indexing? No. It's an argument for having a very real and sobering respect for the power of financial markets. The securities markets aren't an amorphous and faceless shadow; they represent the faith and works of *people*. When we say "the markets," we mean four of them—the stock, bond, currency, and commodity markets. Trends in these markets are driven by supply and demand; supply and demand is driven by individual emotion and psychology. Being unable to count the denizens of the earth, should we then presume to know in advance what the sum of their actions will be at any given time? To do so would be a violation of natural law.

One of the fundamental laws of quantum phenomena says we can only know one of two things at once about any given particle: where it is, or what size it is. We can't know both, at least not simultaneously. Similarly, we can look at securities markets and immediately deduce one of two things at any given time: *what* is happening, and *why* it is happening. But to determine both simultaneously is an impossibility, unless we're an insider or have specialized knowledge of one narrow sector of the markets.

Does this mean that all market analysis—fundamental or technical—is useless? No. Far from it. But it does mean that no comprehensive system exists for consistently timing the market. To do so would be to invent the perpetual motion machine. Realizing this truth alone allows investors—particularly those saving for retirement—to pursue the simplest strategy: establishing a specific plan and evaluating it continually, rather than monitoring day-to-day price changes continually. The old saying holds true today: Time in the market, rather than timing the market, is the most important ingredient in the recipe for long-term performance.

To do:

- Look at a stock you own and watch its buy and sell orders trade on a Level II quote screen. This screen allows you to see the bid (buy) and ask (sell) prices on the stock in real time. http://www.level2stockquotes.com/level-ii-quotes.html
- Get a copy of Nicolas Darvas' classic, called *How I Made $2,000,000 in the Stock Market*. Darvas, a ballroom dancer who studied the markets for many years, made his money in the fifties and sixties, decades before the technology or housing bubbles. You can get it here on Amazon: http://www.amazon.com/How-Made-000-Stock-Market/dp/0818403969
- Visit the mutual fund screener on Zacks.com. Calculate the S & P's annual return from the beginning of the year to when you bought this book, then the 1, 3, 5, and 10-year returns. Then

use the screener to find out how many mutual funds, on average, consistently outperformed the S & P. http://www.zacks.com/stock/screener/stock-screener.php?type=MFS

Misconception:

Bargains don't exist anymore in the markets.

Reality:

There will never be a market where securities only trade for exactly what they're worth. All commerce would instantly cease because it would be impossible to make a profit.

Proof:

The standard method of valuing securities is based on some kind of periodic payment—a dividend—and its expected growth rate in the future. Typically, an investor's required rate of return will determine how much he or she will pay for a specific investment. If they don't need to earn much, they don't mind paying more. If they want to earn a great deal, they need to pay much less.

We calculate returns on everything we buy—homes, cars, computers. We do it for groceries. One of the oldest saws about the stock market is eerily accurate—it's the only market in the world where everyone is scared to buy when there's an enormous sale.

The average dividend yield of the S & P 500 stocks was 1.84% as of 7 September 2010. This means that, had you put in $100,000 into the index, you would have received $1,840 as a dividend for the 12 months prior. So what is the S & P 500 "worth?" Well, if we take the formula we previously used for preferred stocks, using a required rate of return of 7%, we could say that it's worth $26,285. This is a gross oversimplification, but if we use it, the market is way overvalued.

The problem is that the dividend isn't the only component of how much the stock makes for you—for this we have the earnings per share (EPS). According to data provided by Robert Shiller, Bloomberg, and S & P, the year-end earnings on the S & P 500 were \$83.66 per "share"—that is, the weighted average of the earnings of the 500 businesses making up the index.

So what is this worth to us now? Well, if we divide the \$83.66 by .07 again, we get 1,195.14—a little more than 60 points below the 2010 closing price of 1,257.64 for .SPX. In this case, we'd say the S & P was trading at year-end at 1,257.64/1,195.14 = 105% of its fair value.

"Exactly!" you say. "There aren't any more bargains!" But now let's look at the end of 2008. Here, earnings on the index were \$65.39. Using our required rate of return of 7% again, we get a fair value of .SPX of (65.39/.07) = 934.14. At year's end, the index closed at 903.25. This year, the market was undervalued—it was selling for by 903.25/934.14 = 96.69% of fair value.

OK, big deal. We got a 3% discount. All that does is prove the misconception is true, right? Wrong. Why? Because we can look throughout the year to see what the market sold at. Peeking at the highs and lows for 2008, we see that .SPX traded as high as 1471.77 (157.55% of fair value—expensive!) and as low as 741.02 (79.33% of fair value, or at a 20.67% *discount*—cheap!)

Let's look at this second date, which occurred in November 2008. If we bought here, we would have bought 934.14 worth of assets for 741.02, an over 20% discount. That's a decent bargain, without us doing much work! (If you want bigger bargains, you might have to work harder.)

From this last perspective, the market is undervalued and should be bought. Note also that as this required rate of return decreases (we can use 6%, or 5%, instead of 7%) the intrinsic value of the market rises. Real security value, like beauty, is very much in the eye of the beholder.

To do:

- Look at the earnings per share on the components of the S & P 500. You can find them here: http://pages.stern.nyu.edu/~adamodar/New_Home_Page/datafile/spearn.htm
- Look at your own investments and calculate your own rate of return for a long-term time period, possibly since you started.

- Use this as your required rate of return. Now look at a stock or other security you're thinking of buying. Use its annual dividend as the numerator and your return as the denominator. What value do you get?

Misconception:

Asset allocation doesn't work anymore.

Reality:

Asset allocation with assets that have minimal or negative correlations with each other continues to work, and work beautifully. The challenge is finding minimal and negative correlation.

Proof:

When people complain about losing money in their accounts, they're complaining about something called *standard deviation*—the tendency for an asset to fluctuate from its historical average return. The formula for standard deviation involves a figure called the *correlation coefficient*, which is a measure of its return compared to the return of another asset in a portfolio.

This doesn't need to be mathematical. Essentially, an asset that's perfectly correlated with another asset has a correlation coefficient of 1. A perfectly *negatively* correlated asset has a correlation coefficient of -1. This is what we want. Why? Because the downward movement of one asset in the portfolio is perfectly offset by the upward movement of the negatively correlated asset in the portfolio.

Of course, most asset combinations don't work so neatly. The only way to really achieve perfect negative correlation in most accounts is to buy and sell short the same asset at the same time. This is a perfect "hedge"—the rise in price will benefit the long side, offsetting the loss on the short side. Most assets have different correlation coefficients to one another, which can be intuitively grasped while looking at price patterns on charts.

One such example can be found by looking at a five-year chart of month-by-month prices of the spot price of gold vs. the Japanese yen. If you're looking at this chart, you don't need a calculator to see that the yen falls as the price of gold rises, and vice versa. The two crossed paths in January 2008, vying for mastery, and then did so again in October 2008, as the yen fell and gold soared as investors flocked to it during the world financial crisis.

Another interesting five-year chart is gold vs. the Dow Jones Industrial Average, the most widely followed stock indicator in the US. The correlation isn't quite as symmetrically negative as the yen, but again, you can see that there is a very neat (and, if you're looking to make some money, somewhat predictable) negative correlation between these assets. This negative correlation held until February 2009, a month before the low in the stock market. At this point, both gold and the Dow rallied, exhibiting a *positive* correlation with each other for over a year.

Part of the problem with traditional models for many financial portfolios is that the correlation coefficients between the three traditional asset classes—stocks, bonds, and cash—are becoming closer to 1. The solution isn't arguing that asset allocation doesn't work anymore; the solution is to seek and practice a better definition of asset allocation. Traditionally, there are four asset classes, and they have to be clearly defined: stocks, bonds, currencies, and commodities.

Stocks include domestic and foreign businesses, whether in developed or developing foreign nations. Bonds include foreign and domestic government, corporate, and municipal debt of all maturities, credit ratings, tax status, and interest rates. Currencies can be extremely useful in more efficiently balancing portfolios and are one of the most underused assets in retail asset management. The most widely traded include the yen, Canadian and Australian dollars, the Euro, and the sterling. Finally, commodities typically include the metals—gold, silver, platinum and palladium; energy like crude oil and natural gas; and agricultural products like soybeans, corn, and wheat.

If you do the work to analyze the price movements of these various assets, you may come to one grossly oversimplified conclusion: hard assets and financial assets don't move in tandem. They typically peak and fall at different times, and these peaks and valleys very often offset one another.

Taking account for this fact is a necessity for any successful implementation of asset allocation today.

To do:

- Go back to www.stockcharts.com and access the bar or line charts under the "Free Charts" section. Plot the five year chart of the Japanese yen vs. gold. What do you see? How do these assets appear to correlate—i.e. move in symmetry to one an0ther?
- Replace the yen with the Dow Jones Industrial Average. What does the movement look like now?
- Ask your planner to tell you the correlation coefficients of some of the assets in your portfolio. If it's close to 1, ask them how this number can be improved.

TAX PLANNING

Misconception:

I SHOULD ALWAYS convert my traditional IRA to a Roth IRA.

Reality:

Although many investors stand to benefit from the generous provisions in tax law allowing them to delay paying the full taxes due on Roth conversions until April 2013, investors who are unable to part with the cash to pay the tax up front may be better waiting it out.

Proof:

The argument for the future value of a present dollar is greatly dependent on what return the investor can make. If someone is making 7% on their assets, then $100,000 today is worth $196,000 ten years from now. If they're making 15%, the same $100,000 is worth $404,000. This fact points to one criteria in any decision on whether or not to convert: what return on investment the client a) wants to use; and b) has historically gotten.

It boils down to this: the higher the rate of return, the more beneficial a conversion may be. The reason is that the future value calculations can be applied to tax dollars taken out of the account a) now; and b) when distributions begin. Consider the example above. If the investor was in the 25% tax bracket and decided to convert immediately, they would pay $25,000 on the initial $100,000. If they decided to wait until the account matured and leave it alone, the total tax they would pay on a lump sum distribution would be $49,000—almost twice as much. If the account had actually returned 15%, they would have paid $101,000 in taxes! The federal government well knows that tax dollars—the dollars they get—can compound at the same rate as the non-taxed dollars—the dollars the investor gets. Think of the Roth IRA conversion initiative from the IRS' perspective—a way to collect substantial sums of tax revenue now, rather than waiting for distribution dollars that typically come out piecemeal over IRA holder's lifetimes.

Of course, this very same fact may prevent an IRA holder from considering a conversion—the fact that they'll *never* take a lump sum distribution. Knowing well that they may die before the IRS life expectancy tables are betting they will, holders of traditional IRAs need not (they tell themselves) worry about ever having to pay the whole tax, because they'll never take it all out. This is a valid consideration, and may induce investors to consider a partial Roth conversion, or none at all.

But the most important considerations are straightforward ones: assets and age. A 29-year-old with a traditional IRA with $5,000 and a 68-year-old with $750,000 can both consider a Roth conversion, but they won't have the same experience. The 29-year-old has three decades of compounding ahead of him; the 68-year-old has to begin taking money out in two years' time. If the former has a 15% effective tax rate and the latter has a 28% effective tax rate, they would pay $750 and $210,000, respectively. Why is age important? Again, because of compounding. If the 29-year-old sinks just the minimum contribution in per year and earns 7%, he'll have over $530,000 tax-free—almost as much as the 68-year-old has at conversion! The 68-year-old simply doesn't have the same amount of time that the 29-year-old has.

Assets have a double meaning here: not only assets in the account, but any assets available may be liquidated and used to pay the tax. If the 68-year-old has no other financial or liquid assets, he may well sit the opportunity out to convert; let the account remain a traditional IRA. The Roth conversion opportunity is a tremendous one for many and even possibly most traditional IRA holders—it allows a two-year window to pay the tax. But it's not a great deal for everyone. It's critical, as the world of finance becomes more complex, that you make every informed attempt to make sure that you and your beneficiaries, not the Treasury, stand the most to gain from your decision.

To do:

- Ask your planner for a Roth IRA conversion illustration. Ask them to explain it to you.
- Ask your planner what the tax consequence would be if you: a) paid the tax in full in the year of conversion; and b) paid it over the window between now and April 2013 that the IRS permits.
- Ask your planner, or figure out yourself, what your annualized rate of return has been on your investments since you began them. This will give you an idea of what you've been earning since you began. (Hint: accounts with losses typically make better candidates for Roth conversions; the sum on which tax is levied is smaller.)

Misconception:

Tax-free bonds are enough.

Reality:

Every investor objective is different, but even wealthy income investors may sometimes be better served by taxable investments.

Proof:

The case for tax-free debt is strong. According to figures from Franklin Templeton, municipal bonds had the highest after-tax total return of any asset class except stocks for the 20-year period ending 12.31.2006. Other factors should improve these standings going forward, like the potential return of the 39.6% federal income tax bracket in 2013. (At the last minute, just before the rates would have risen in 1.1.11, in December 2010, President Obama and Congress lengthened the 2001 EGTRRA tax brackets through 12.31.2012.)

Despite all this, many municipal investments are sold without any regard whatever to the client's actual tax bracket. More commonly, these funds are left alone in client accounts with the assumption that these brackets never change. Finally, as is the case with many business clients of accountants, the feeling often seems to be that *less* income that *hasn't* been taxed is—amazingly—preferable to *more* income that *has* been. In other words, some business people have such a virulent hatred of federal, state and local levies that they prefer $10 that's non-taxable to $12 after tax.

Does this sound incredible? I know it's true, because I've proposed changes in client investments along these lines. For example, one friend of mine had two municipal funds. Their tax-free yields were 3.08% and 3.31%, respectively. At the highest bracket at the time, the taxable equivalent yields would have been 4.73% and 5.09%. The investment I was proposing had a taxable equivalent yield of 7%, with no difference in credit quality.

It wasn't an easy sale—the client had his accountant review the information and (reluctantly) agreed to go forward after getting the word back from him. Why did this client have a difficult time with the proposal? He was concerned about risk, for one, which was understandable. We're taught never to expect something for nothing. But the second—and somewhat unspoken—reason was that the debt would be taxable. Furthermore, the client wasn't in the top bracket—he was in the 25% marginal bracket! The taxable equivalent yields here were only 4.10% and 4.41%. Perhaps doubling his yield without changing the credit risk of the issues seemed too good to be true.

The assertion that an investor needs nothing more than tax-free debt is also a violation of Modern Portfolio Theory. This theory, introduced by Harry Markowitz in the early 1950s, maintains that multiple asset classes with low and negative correlations to each other will be needed to achieve a well-diversified portfolio. Since bonds don't move in exact lockstep with currencies, stocks, and commodities, making them the sole asset class in any portfolio will make the investor susceptible to far wider swings than a balanced portfolio.

To do:

- Review any tax-free investments in your portfolio. What are the tax-free yields?
- Look at your W-2. Look at the tax you paid compared to your taxable income. Divide the first by the second. This is your *effective* tax rate.

- Divide the tax-free yields of your investments by (1 - the effective tax rate as a decimal). So, for example, if your effective rate was 25% and you have tax-free bonds yielding 5%, you'd get 5% /(1 - .25) = 6.67%. This is your *taxable equivalent yield*—the yield you have to get on a taxable investment to match what you're making. How does it compare to the other yields you've seen out there?

Misconception:

I'll never get audited.

Reality:

Depending on their income, eighty-nine to ninety-nine out of 100 people that say this are right. The rest are wrong.

Proof:

According to the IRS, there were 236,503,000 tax returns filed in the US in 2009. Of these, 182,522,000 of them were for income taxes. The rest were for estate, employment, gift, and other types of taxes, as well as tax-exempt groups and excise taxes. Of the income tax entities, the breakdown looks something like the following:

C or other corporations: 2,476,000
S corps—4,496,000
Partnerships—3,565,000
Individuals—144,103,000
Individuals (estimated tax)—24,197,000
Estates and trusts—3,143,000
Estates and trusts (estimated tax)—542,000

All right, so it isn't *Die Hard 4*. This is, after all, tax data. Now let's look at the percentage of these returns that were examined, which is essentially either the first step to an audit. We'll look directly at the percentage of returns that were examined by the IRS grouped by adjusted gross income. They are:

No AGI—4.04%		
$1—$24,999—.97%		
$25,000—$49,999—.7%		
$50,000—$74,999—.68%		
$75,000—$99,999—.57%		
$100,000—$199,999—.67%		
$200,000—$499,999—1.86%		
$500,000—$999,999—2.77%		
$1MM—$4,999,999—5.35%		
$5MM—$9,999,999—7.52%		
$10MM+ — 10.60%		

Do you see the trends? The edges—those filers with the very highest and lowest (actually, none) AGI are the ones who are likeliest to be audited. Middle income taxpayers—those with some AGI under $200,000—are less likely to be audited. Income tax returns with AGI between $1 and $200,000 make up 95.55% of those required to file, so it's safe to say that your chance of an audit here is between .67% and .97%—less than 1 in a hundred.

So where am I getting 89 to 99 out of 100, as asserted, above? Well, it depends on which 100 people you ask. If you're in a roomful of accredited investors, all of which make at least $200,000 a year, the odds of audit double, triple, or multiply tenfold. For a party suite at the Waldorf-Astoria with 100 of the richest Americans celebrating New Year's, the odds increase to better than one in ten. (If you include the ones that are clever enough to declare no AGI, then they're more like one in seven.)

IRS examinations are fairly straightforward and come in three degrees. The first and simplest, called a correspondence examination, is handled through the mail or by phone and typically focuses only on a few items on the return. The second type, called an office examination, requires the filer to visit an IRS district office to address a tax auditor's queries about specific items on the return. Finally, the most comprehensive of the three is the field examination, where a revenue agent meets a filer at his office, home, or accountant's office.

If you are audited, your accountant is the first one to contact. He or she is always the best one to speak to concerning any items you may not understand or remember concerning your returns. One general rule that's applicable—in life as well as in finance—is that the truth is always the easiest thing to remember.

To do:

- Ask your CPA how vulnerable you are to an audit or examination. Is there anything you can do to minimize this risk?
- If you have a business or are self-employed, your risk of audit increases substantially, according to IRS figures. Repeating the question above to your accountant, are you satisfied with the answer?
- In the slight chance that an audit brings up something unfavorable that wasn't your fault, find out if your CPA or attorney is appointed to practice before the IRS. This is a special status the IRS grants to certain parties, usually accountants, lawyers, and actuaries. You may never use it, but it might come in handy one day. If your professional isn't appointed to practice, do they know someone who is?

Misconception:

My CPA knows everything.

Reality:

There's too much information in even one sector of finance for anyone to know everything.

Proof:

Financial planning has eight fundamental practice areas: education, employee benefit, and estate planning, financial statement preparation & analysis, investment, retirement, & tax planning, and risk management/insurance. Let's pick one area—say retirement planning. If we choose this discipline, we find that we can subdivide it into about ten different areas. These are:

• Determining the retirement need
• Government-sponsored plans (Social Security, Medicare, etc.)
• Personal savings plans
• Employer-sponsored plans
• Qualified plans
• Defined contribution plans
• Defined benefit plans
• Distributions
• Regulation
• Choosing a plan for a business

Each of these topics can be further broken down. For example, personal savings plans can be broken down into traditional IRAs, Roth IRAs, and annuities. Let's focus on the first topic—traditional IRAs only. A simple examination of how much material exists on this simple topic is eye-opening. If you wanted to know everything about this topic alone, a healthy start would include these publications:

• Publication 590, from the IRS—130 pps
• The Pension Protection Act—contains specific newer laws touching on IRAs—394 pps
• Subsection 408, Subpart A, Part I, Subchapter D, Chapter 1, Subtitle A, Title 26, United States Code—15 pps
• IRS Revenue Rulings 2004-12, 2002-62, 1992-47, 1989-89, 1989-50, 1987-77, 1986-78, 1986-142, 1984-146, 1982-153—43 pps
• Taxation of Individual retirement Accounts, 2010—1200 pps

Even a cursory look at these publications indicates the depth and complexity of them. And each area has sub-areas! This is not to denigrate the professional abilities of the tax, legal, and financial advisors that focus on specific areas—typically, the best-known names focus on just one area. Suze Orman focuses on credit and liability management for the working woman. Ed Slott—"America's IRA Expert"—focuses on minimizing tax liability for those with assets in IRAs and retirement plans. Jim Cramer's encyclopedic knowledge of the business fundamentals of many (most?) publicly traded stocks is legendary. But none of them knows everything.

As always: how does this impact you? Well, in the first place, don't be overawed by letters after someone's name. It's true, they can be a good indicator of the advisor's general knowledge. But, in all honesty, do you expect your advisor to know everything? There are over 2,000 financial designations available in the marketplace today. They range from the very simple, in which a few hour's study and an online test (with a fee) can get you certified, to a 6-month to 2-4+ year study program with in-depth and full-time education. All designations aren't created equally! And neither do they provide the same expertise to the client.

Secondly, gauge whether or not the advisor will level with you. If you ask a detailed question and they give you an answer that you sense or know is wrong, you know something's not right. "I don't know" is a perfectly acceptable answer, but many planners are afraid to say it. You should want to hear this answer, as well as its corollary, "but I'll find out and get back to you with the answer."

Finally: don't assume! If you ask a question when faced with a decision, make sure you're comfortable! Not knowing the facts and trusting your advisor isn't a problem. But not knowing the facts and having any doubts whatsoever about your advisor is a problem. Make sure that you either understand the transaction proposed, as well as its benefit to you, or that you trust this advisor with your life. Better yet, both.

To do:

- Ask yourself what areas of your financial life (from the eight above) are the most pressing for you. If necessary, put them in a list, prioritizing them.
- Talk to your planner, CPA, or legal advisor about these areas and ask them for additional names of people they know that concentrate on these areas.
- Ask these professionals questions and use your intuition! Are they hedging, or are they straightforward?

Misconception:

My CPA doesn't know *anything*.

Reality:

Your advisor—tax, legal, financial, or other—had to pass at least one or two specialized tests to legally be allowed to dispense paid advice in the first place.

Proof:

The FINRA Series 7 exam is the most comprehensive exam offered for representatives to offer securities to the general public. It's also the simplest of the three major tests corresponding to law, finance, and accounting.

Two-thirds (66%) of test takers pass the exam the first time; the average score is 73. The test is divided among various sections, most prominent among them stocks, government, corporate and municipal bonds, options, limited partnerships, mutual funds, and securities regulations. It is administered in two 3-hour sessions; each session has 130 questions (125 of which count towards the test). Bottom line: if your broker passed it, he's probably not an orangutan.

If, as mentioned in the last note, your advisor has letters after her name, the odds continue to drop that she doesn't know what she's talking about. The function of education and regulation in any profession—including professional standards to be upheld—are to ensure that the members of the public availing themselves of these services are protected against *risk*. This is why medical school lasts four years—the most schooling has to be accorded those who have the most power (and thus responsibility) over their fellows. Performing open heart surgery involves risk at the highest level. The answer to this is found in *testing*—in formally assessing someone's level of knowledge of a required procedure. You pass the test, you can take your Hippocratic oath. You don't, you pick another line of work.

Lawyers also incur significant risk, particularly trial lawyers. The knowledge that your research, ability to communicate, and fighting spirit could mean the difference between someone's wrongful imprisonment or death—and their exoneration—commands an element of awe. It also can mean confidence for the client—even the public defenders had to pass the bar!

Next in the lineup is finance. Though the risks here aren't life-threatening, they can certainly be *lifestyle*-threatening. Saying "sure you can!" to a client who wants to take out 10% of their IRA a year and have it last forever—that's lifestyle-threatening. Buying too much of one stock without any risk management—that's lifestyle-threatening. Failing to make provisions for a breadwinner client's premature demise—that's lifestyle-threatening.

Take heart. Although financial planners are far closer to salespeople than medical doctors or attorneys, the system of testing and regulations in place—and constantly being innovated on—is a very healthy start in making sure that your advisor is competent and able to fulfill their duty of care to you.

To do:

- Take a look at the content outline of the Series 7 exam on FINRA's website. You can find it here: http://www.finra.org/web/groups/industry/@ip/@comp/@regis/documents/industry/p038201.pdf
- Now compare an outline of the content of the CPA exam. To find this, go here: http://www.aicpa.org/BecomeACPA/CPAExam/ExaminationContent/ContentAndSkills/DownloadableDocuments/CSOs-SSOs-Final-Release-Version-effective-01-01-2011.pdf
- Next—you guessed it—comes the bar exam. Look at the content topics here for the bar for New York State: http://www.nybarexam.org/Docs/CONTENT%20OUTLINE%20(revised%20May%202010).pdf

Misconception:

Taxes are a curse on any free society.

Reality:

Taxes pay for nearly every good public benefit in existence, particularly for those who are unable to provide them for themselves.

Proof:

The federal government collected approximately $2.1 trillion in tax revenue in 2009. Of this, 43% was in individual income tax, another 42% was in Social Security/insurance tax, and 7% was from corporate tax. Federal spending, however, was not quite twice receipts—$3.5 trillion for the same time period. Social Security and Medicare made up 39% of this sum, or $1.35 trillion, compared to the $891 billion in taxes collected for these programs. If anything, there aren't *enough* taxes collected to cover the payment of these benefits.

It seems hard to believe, especially in a society where the average working person doesn't ever seem to be able to get enough take-home pay. But ask the 12,000 or so people that turn 62 every day in the United States if they really are sorry for the Social Security tax. According to Elaine Floyd of Horsesmouth, a New York financial research and advisory firm, the average lifetime benefit of someone who began receiving the maximum monthly amount in 2008 was $298,000 over the ensuing decade, $690,000 over the next two decades, and over $1.2 million for the following 30 years.

There's an ancient saying enjoining the Jewish people to praise their God for "granting you peace on your frontiers" (Psalm 147.14). There are others to thank, too, though—namely, the 1.42 million or so members of the Army, Navy, Air Force, Marines, and Coast Guard. About 23 cents of every dollar in taxes collected goes to defense spending; the Department of Defense's base budget is $533.8 billion. The remaining $240+ billion is generally divided between Veterans Affairs, Homeland Security, nuclear weapons maintenance, and the State Department. Despite the fervid controversy over the Iraq War and the ongoing criticism of foreign policy of the Bush administration by many, there seem to be relatively few in power advising curtailment of the nation's armed forces. On the contrary, Secretary of Defense Robert Gates requested (and received) an increase in the amount of military personnel by 2012, especially in the Army and Marine Corps. President Obama proposed a 4% increase in defense spending in 2011, followed by a 9% decrease in 2012. All of these programs are funded by taxes.

While there are other areas where tax dollars are usefully spent, it may be this area—defense—is the most overlooked. Happily, most who criticize the military aren't leveling invective at the soldiers or marines themselves; they're leveling the policymakers' use of them. Unfortunately, many take the stand that the military itself should be stripped or even dismantled; that everything should be handled through dialogue and diplomacy. But ask those same people to walk through the worst neighborhoods in the country at night without a police escort or weapon; will they be as critical of defense policy afterward? Doubtful.

To do:

- Look at your pay stub and find out how much FICA tax you paid this pay period. Figure out how much you paid for the whole year.
- Now get your Social Security statement and see what your benefit will be at the three various ages. Without doing extensive calculations, multiply that amount by 120, 240, and 360. This is a (very!) crude estimate of what you'll receive from the program (without adjusting for inflation) over 10, 20, and 30 years.
- Look at your earnings record on the same statement, year over year. Average the years out and multiply that amount, by the number of years you've worked, by .062. This is another (very!) crude estimate of the Social Security tax you've paid into the system. Compare what you've paid in, to what you're estimated to receive out. (Also note: for 2011-2012, this figure falls from .062 to .042. But for the calculation, use .062—this is what you've been contributing for pretty much all your working life to date.)

Misconception:

Quickbooks is enough.

Reality:

The financial services industry is taking a beating, and the direction is leaning towards *more* documentation, not less.

Proof:

One of the first stories I heard as a trainee was from a wirehouse sales manager at my first job on Wall Street. I still see him now, similar to the bespectacled, wizened Yogi Berra-like creature giving Tom Cruise such good advice in *Jerry Maguire*. The story was about a financial planner who had opened accounts with a businessman from the Western New York area, who experienced a loss, and who then took the planner to arbitration. Since the notetaking had been less than perfect on the part of the planner, it was his word vs. the client's. Walking into the arbitration room, the planner watched in disbelief as his client—whom he had spent numerous hours with in detailed review of his portfolio—began speaking heatedly in Italian, motioning to the panel that he couldn't speak English.

This was a lie, the manager told us. But the planner was unable to defend himself, in part because he hadn't taken sufficient notes. Auditors have limited materials to look at when they review material, and most of what they do review is pieces of paper. If you use Quickbooks or other forms of accounting software, you've made a good investment in your own financial reporting system. But it never hurts to err on the side of caution when it comes to keeping financial and tax records, records of client communications and meetings, and any other pertinent financial data. Corporate and nonprofit boards highlight and often italicize and bold-type decisions and actions taken at meetings in their minutes. Should you do less when monitoring your own financial decisions and interactions with your planner?

"I'm never going to sue my planner," you say. "I don't need that." Believe it or not, your notes may help you *protect* your planner, if they're truly acting in your best interest. I've been on the receiving end of calls from overzealous attorneys, who make much of their living convincing clients to sue their advisors for losses in their accounts and errors in financial planning projections. (Of the two calls I've received, both were about clients' previous advisors, before they began work with me.) This is serious stuff! Any complaint goes on a planner's U-4, and any arbitration proceeding will stay with that planner for a long time to come. One thing the attorneys look for is uncertainty—if they ask the client a fairly detailed question and they don't have any idea what the answer is. In one case, the call led to an arbitration hearing, where I was subpoenaed as a witness on behalf of the client against the previous advisor. I was subpoenaed for my notes, which I had taken electronically after meeting with this client for the first few times. Good notes mean proper procedure for a planner, and a clearer understanding and comfort for the client. They can also mean money for the attorneys.

In the second case, a third party law firm approached my client—I don't know how. They had a conversation with him and called me for information. The thrust of it was that the previous advisor had given this client retirement planning projections that were created prior to 2008 and were therefore—you guessed it—unrealistically high. (To be fair, I didn't see them, so I don't know what they projected.)

Had these clients themselves taken notes of the interactions they had had with their advisors, they might have avoided any legal wrangling in the first place. One of the common pieces of advice given for anyone who wants to become a straight A student is to take copious notes while learning something new. The second piece is to review those notes as soon after learning as possible. (The third is my favorite, which is to get 8 hours' good sleep a night—I definitely sleep like a straight A student.) When depositing part or all of your life savings with someone, do you want to "get an A?" Then one of you should be taking a lot of notes—either you or the planner. Doing so can help not only you, but them.

To do:

- Ask if your planner has notes from your previous meetings and how they record them.
- Look through your records and see if you have notes of your meetings with your planner. Review them. Are they comprehensible?
- Ask for your loved one to conduct an informal "audit" of your business or financial papers. Are you a "low-risk" auditee? Or could your documentation skills use some work?

Misconception:

A gain I have to pay taxes on is worse than no gain at all.

Reality:

Half of something is something, and none of nothing is still nothing. The only question answered is: do you want something, or nothing?

Proof:

Does this need proving? If a client buys an investment and it doubles, the client has a 100% gain before taxes. Even if taxes are 50%, the client still nets 50%. That's the cost of democracy. It's staggering to me that market conditions can illuminate when the right time to sell is, all the stars can be aligned, and the client still doesn't sell—because he doesn't want to take a tax hit. Paying 15% in taxes is worse to them than receiving 85% of the gains they've gotten.

So how does this scenario play out in real life? "Don't sell yet. I don't want to pay the tax." OK, fine. But what if we're at a peak, and the reason I called you was to tell you we should take some profits? Your decision could be to take 50% of the profit you have now, or lose half that profit—or more. So if we bought at $50,000 and you made $50,000, that means you'd net $25,000. If the investment falls to $75,000, that means the gain is now $12,500. Yes, Washington will get $12,500 less. But you'd rather have $12,500 less too?

This is the half-empty glass at its worst. Taxes are a bill, like any other bill; you put them on the cash flow statement like any other expense. But for some reason the inward pull is much tighter, much more difficult to deal with. We don't begrudge the power company, or the auto manufacturer, or the cable company when we pay. We look at the bill, make sure it isn't crazy, and pay it. But taxes are different, aren't they? The people in Washington don't know what they're doing—they just fight to get there, and then they just work to stay there. They aren't using the tax revenue right; they don't deserve the money. Why give it to them?

Because you have to.

If you feel as though you're going to have a heart attack every time your planner sells something at a gain, or when you're about to make a profitable trade, tell yourself that even though the government gets part of it, your part is usually bigger. Make sure your accountant is using all the deductions available to you, especially the miscellaneous itemized deductions. Make sure your accountant is helping you make full use of any deductions, credits, or other benefits available to you if you have portfolio or passive income.

Don't underestimate the power of trading and aggressive investing in qualified (pretax) accounts. This is the place to take gains; you can hold your 50% trading profit up high and say to the IRS (with apologies to M.C. Hammer) "Can't Touch This." These are mainly your IRA. If you feel the need or urge to take profit and the thought of taxes being paid revulses you, make the trade in your IRA or 401(k). Sell and take profits there first, then countenance the thought of trading your taxable account.

Finally, if you have investments that have significant tax consequences for selling, make sure you have a good team! Ensure your accountant and attorney are competent in minimizing estate, income, and other major liabilities you may be exposed to. Their goals should be aligned with yours fully in reducing the actual tax you pay, both in life and in death.

To do:

- Call your planner and have her examine your investments—all of them. Ask her if there are any positions she thinks you should sell, regardless of tax consequences.
- Call your CPA and ask him what the tax consequences of selling those investments would be.
- Call your attorney and ask what the ramifications for your estate are.

Misconception:

I've got the expenses in my head.

Reality:

The old saw from the newspaper business holds true: the dullest pencil is sharper than the keenest memory. Write them down!

Proof:

One of the first tests that can help someone who always seems to run out of money before the end of the month is the receipt test. It isn't as sophisticated as it sounds. 1. Get a paper bag. 2. Save the receipt from every single purchase you make for 30 days. 3. Stick them in the bag. 4. Look and see how much you spent at the end of the 30 days.

Doing this will open almost anyone's eyes. Do you really know what you spend on food? What you spend eating out? What you spend on Amazon and iTunes? Clothing? Auto detailing? Your favorite hobby?

A typical statement of cash flows will have twelve major categories: housing, utilities, food, auto, medical, clothing, insurance, taxes, appliances, personal care, recreation, and miscellaneous. Of these twelve, how many are fairly easy to predict month by month? Housing and utilities, auto and (hopefully) medical, taxes and appliances. The rest are the "money pit" for most individuals, and they vary by personality. A thirty-something single woman in midtown Manhattan will generally be more inclined to shop for clothing than a married forty-something in the Midwest. An eighteen-year-old rock music aficionado will rack up more downloads than most university professors in their sixties. The point is that, very often, more money goes out than comes in—and the person who spent it has no idea where.

One of the best examples is a beverage that's been around since the tenth century—coffee. Dunkin Donuts serves about 30 cups per second. In the US, 100 million people drink coffee a day; they average 3.4 cups apiece. Of these cups, 2.3 are gourmet. That means that 67% of coffee consumed each day is purchased from a gourmet outlet. Now, granted that many of these gourmet outlets are from consumers buying coffee in bags and brewing it at home—77% of coffee consumption is in the house. But the average cost for those who buy by the cup is $2 for traditional coffee and $4-5 for specialty coffee at Starbucks, according to July 2007 figures. Coffee Research's figures estimate that in 1999, the average American consumer spent $164.71 per annum on coffee.

This is no king's ransom. But if this is an average price, then many are spending more than this amount each year. Simply buying more coffee and keeping it at home could halve this amount; and, more importantly, create a habit of discipline for the household who is presumably trying to maximize discretionary income.

To do:

- If you don't want to take the receipts test, pay for everything you buy in the next week by credit or debit card. Then review your statement at month end.
- What expense category do you tend to spend the most on? Does it generally vary?
- If you're surprised at the results, try tracking expenses more closely with the receipts test for 30 days.

Misconception:

I'm taking as much as I can under the table.

Reality:

The combination of audit risk, lack of federal entitlement income, and the loss of retirement savings programs more than offset "more in the pocket" for most taxpayers.

Proof:

Under-the-table income is the most common way for waiters, bellhops, cab drivers, doormen, and thousands of other individuals to earn their living. Unfortunately, it's also the one most susceptible to the risk of an audit by the IRS. While the risk still isn't very high—the typical percentage of returns audited are closer to 1% than 2%—the possibility, accompanied by a tax penalty that may or may not be in the auditee's savings account, is a deterrent for many.

Another of the major ill effects that untaxed income causes is the lack of payment into federal entitlement programs—Social Security and Medicare. If someone nearing retirement or even in early middle age has gone *around* the system without paying *into* the system, they haven't fooled anyone but themselves. This is because very few programs can match the overall returns that these entitlement programs provide. As mentioned above, someone with the maximum amount of taxable income can receive over $1MM of lifetime income at retirement through Social Security. And, if the number one fear of most individual investors is today is generating current income, a close second is obtaining health insurance. According to the CFP Board's 2009 National Consumer Survey. 55% of respondents said health insurance was a major concern. No other long-term financial concern came close, with the exception of two: building a retirement fund (51%), and preparing for future medical needs (42%).

But maybe the most inimical impact receiving untaxed income has is the illusion of wealth it can create to the recipient. A stream of current income that is abnormally high because of this tax evasion can be extremely satisfying—even exhilarating—to the recipient; but without a savings program it is only as reliable as the individual's health and circumstances. The median 401(k) balance in the US, for example, was $43,700 as of October 2009, according to the Employee Benefit Research Institute. The bulk of these plans are fed by automated payroll deductions into the investment options inside the plans—mutual funds, annuities, stocks, etc. In other words, the employees aren't making a conscious decision to budget a percentage of their pay and invest it; it's being done for them.

In this case, those who are being paid under the table have to make a conscious decision to save, which requires tremendous discipline. The knowledge that IRS penalties and taxes will be levied on 401(k) and other retirement plan distributions is a significant psychological barrier for many. Without these barriers, it's questionable that someone saving money in a non-retirement account would have the discipline to save as long. If a 50-year-old invests the full $22,000 permissible for 2010 until retirement at age 65 and earns 8% on their funds, they'll have nearly $600,000—all tax-deferred. Is it likely someone getting this much under the table would be able to contribute so much, defer so much, and keep their hot little hands off so much? Probably not.

To do:

- Ask your planner what options there are for retirement plans, particularly what the limits are. Pay particular attention to the maximum deferral amounts.
- Ask your planner to do an estimate of how much you could accumulate at retirement if you deferred the maximum amount and made a fixed percentage.
- Take the same contribution amount and time period, but now multiply your rate of return by (1-your tax bracket). This is your after-tax rate of return—the amount of money you'll make if you bank it without paying tax in the first place. How does it compare?

RETIREMENT PLANNING

Misconception:

I 'M TAKING MY Social Security at 62; it won't even be there when I'm 70.

Reality:

The long-term solvency of the Social Security trust funds is directly proportionate to the IRS' ability to tax its citizens. For Social Security to vanish, taxing power would have to vanish.

Proof:

Social Security benefits are paid from a tax of 6.20% on covered earnings as of 2010. (For 2011 and 2012, the employee's share of this tax drops to 4.2%.) The self-employed pay 12.5% (10.5% in 2011-2012). According to figures from Buzzle.com, the average annual salary for those 25 years old and above in the US is $43,362. According to the Census Bureau, 65.79% of the US population is above age 25. This translates to 200 million people. If we take the average wage, multiply it by 12.4%, and multiply by this number of people, we get over $108 billion. This is the amount collected in Social Security taxes each year.

The loudest arguments for the insolvency of Social Security come from those who point to the ratio of tax payors to benefit payees. In 1950, it was 16:1, now it's 3.3:1, and by 2030 it will be 2:1. This is accurate, but let's look at the demographics of the country for a moment. According to the

Census Bureau, there were 84.44 million males under age 40 and 80.97 million females under age 40 in 2008. That's 165 million people under 40 in the country—over 54%! These people—all of them—have a minimum of 23 more years to pay into the Social Security system before they're able to receive any benefits. And none of them will attain their full retirement age until they turn 67.

Let's look a little further into the data. Of the under age 40 figures, 31.29 million of the males are under age 15, while 29.81 million of the females are. That number in itself is more than 20% of the country. If you read an article about the Social Security system and become concerned about payor/payee ratios, ask yourself what the life expectancy—and hence the potential tax revenue—is going to be for these youngsters. What will it be by the time they retire? 89? 95? 100?

Finally, the government is able to do something else that it has yet to do—raise the ceiling on the Social Security tax from its current "height" of $106,800. Currently, an individual making $106,800 and another making $2,000,000 pay the same amount of Social Security tax. If Congress changes this law and removes the ceiling—as they have with the Medicare tax—this limit could be removed. This would obviously penalize the highest income-earning Americans significantly, but the government has no problem taxing the rich—even a cursory glance at the estate tax reveals that.

And, while fanciful, the government has even other avenues it could consider. For example, taking away or even modifying the tax exemption on municipal bonds would provide untold millions and possibly billions in tax revenue for the government. (I said it was fanciful.) The government can also take the simple path of least resistance: raise the age benefits are paid, or lower the benefit amounts. Regardless of which direction the government takes, the argument that Social Security won't be there may be the least of your worries—it will mean the government has lost its constitutional power to tax its citizens. French Revolution redux, anyone?

To do:

- Review your Social Security statement and look at your lifetime earnings on it. Take the average of these numbers and multiply by

.062. This is your "lifetime tax yield" to the Treasury. What is it? This is the number you've personally paid in Social Security tax.

- Divide this number by 12. This is the average amount you've paid in per month for your working life.
- Look at your monthly benefit amount. How does the payout compare to the payin?

Misconception:

Annuities are too expensive.

Reality:

Paying an insurance premium to ensure that your money doesn't run out in retirement may provide one of the best emotional returns in financial markets.

Proof:

I have a client who invested with me on October 9, 2007. This was the all-time high of the Dow Jones Industrial Average, to the day. 14,159.65. He had been dissatisfied with his returns at another firm; the fixed income and real estate dividends and interest had made him feel like he couldn't compete with the people he kept hearing about on CNBC. So in one of his two accounts, he went with an all-equity portfolio.

This account started with a value of $302,239.68. (Keep in mind this is an individual retirement account.) The following were the account balances for the next few months:

November 2007 (10.31.07)— $299,020.68
December 2007—$288,142.79
January 2008—$265,174.22
February 2008—$261,988.05
March 2008—$259,958.52

This went on through the disastrous Q4 of 2008, and continued until a low of $155,640.23 was hit—a whopping 48.50% loss from his initial amount. Holding fast, the client was rewarded (somewhat) for his patience, and grew back to $246,684.78 as of May 2010.

Neil Rackham, an author who wrote *SPIN Selling*, described what a successful sales process is built on: S (for situation), P (for problem), I (for implication), and N (for need-payoff). The most important part of this, according to Rackham, is the I—the *implications* of a specific problem. It's not enough to know you have a problem; you have to begin to feel the pain, so to speak, before you'll do anything about it.

Here the implication isn't a declining account balance—month after month after month during that bleak recession. (Incidentally, NBER—National Bureau of Economic Research, the ones who define what a recession is—said as of this writing that the recession officially ended as of June 2009.) The declining account balance is only the *problem*. The *implication*—as this is where the pain begins—is that the retirement paychecks—the "salary" per year out of this account looked like this during the same periods:

November 2007	$14,961.03
December 2007	$14,407.14
January 2008	$13,528.71
February 2008	$13,099.40
March 2008	$12,997.93

And so on, until the low of February 2009—$7,782.01—was hit. This is the implication—having a lifestyle planned around $15,000 from this account, and then having it halved by one wild market.

Should it be evident by now that variable annuities were designed to solve this problem? Even a basic living benefit rider on an annuity would have kept the annual "salary" in this account at the initial level, if not higher—almost $15,000. And many annuities offer more attractive benefits than this.

Interestingly enough, this client declined to purchase an annuity, saying this precise thing—the fees were too high. I'm still not sure why, although I suspect part of it is the fact that he doesn't really need the income now and is unusually patient with respect to financial markets. He has been taught—as we all have—that patience does pay off. But to this day, he won't be able to take as much guaranteed income from his account as he could have if he had initially paid for a living benefit rider. Saying to yourself that you saved 1.5% in fees isn't going to put any extra food on the table in retirement. But a living benefit—in many and even most cases—may.

To do:

- Look at your own account statements and examine the highs and lows between September 2007 and now. What are they like?
- If you don't have an annuity, examine what 5% of your account would have been at each month end. This is what most annuity companies will offer you as a guaranteed income amount. What do the numbers look like?
- Ask your planner to show you what impact a living benefit might have had during this period on your accounts. Does it make sense?

Misconception:

Annuities are too hard to understand.

Reality:

Ask any eight-year old if they want an increase in their allowance. If they say "yes," then they pretty much understand annuities.

Proof:

An annuity is a stream of payments. Technically, your auto note payments are an annuity, your mortgage payments, utility payments, and educational loan payments—all these are annuities. The main difference with the term "annuity" when investing is discussed is that we mean a stream of payments *received* by the investor, not *made* by the investor. This is one of the fundamental desires of those nearing retirement—they want an income that they can rely on, regardless of economic conditions.

Annuities are nothing new—they were sold in one form or another by the ancient Romans, the European nations in the 17th century, and in the United States since the nation's birth. Molly Pitcher, the storied heroine of the Battle of Monmouth pictured bringing cooling water to cannonneers in the Revolutionary War, was awarded an annuity for her acts of patriotism. Various state and even the federal governments financed many Indian land purchases with annuities—they promised lifetime income to the natives in exchange for guaranteed lifetime payments. Most historians agree that many, if not most, of these arrangements were unfair to the Indians.

Annuities come in two main flavors—fixed and variable. Fixed annuities are simple—they're the reverse of life insurance. With life insurance, you pay periodic small payments in and receive a large check at death. With a fixed annuity, you pay a lump sum in during your lifetime and receive periodic payments at your retirement.

Most people intuitively understand this. So where's the confusion? Typically, when people say they don't understand an annuity, they mean a *variable* annuity—one whose values (and, hence, whose payments) fluctuate with the market values of the assets inside it. There are two main ways to take the payments under a variable annuity, and this is what causes most of the confusion. The first way is to annuitize the contract—to give the whole sum of money to the insurer and take payments for the rest of your life (beginning at age 59 1/2 or 60, for most annuities). The second way is to take what are called living benefits—benefits to be obtained for an investor's lifetime, without annuitizing the contract (giving up the money).

Where's the confusion? One you give up the money, one you don't. Well, living benefits, in one sense, sound too good to be true. Typically, they work like this: you buy an annuity contract for $500,000. The annuity company, under a common living benefit, will guarantee you 5% of that, or $25,000 a year, for the rest of your life, provided you abide by contract provisions. (Typically, all this means is that you don't take out more than that amount each year.) Why is it too good to be true? Because, even if you invest aggressively enough to cut your account down to $150,000, you still receive the $25,000 per year—as long as you live.

Most annuity companies add a step-up feature to these contracts—that is, if the market value of the investments goes up more than 5%, you receive a higher guaranteed withdrawal amount the following year. In the above example, suppose the account value, instead of dropping to $150,000, soared to $625,000 (after the $25,000 taken out) on the contract anniversary. If this occurred, the new guaranteed withdrawal amount would be $31,250—a $6,250 increase from last year's pay! This is now the new guaranteed income amount for life, no matter what—even if the contract value subsequently drops to zero.

The most commonly asked question is, "How can the insurance companies afford to do that?" The main answer is, they don't have a net loss on your account until you spend it down to zero. In other words, even if the account described above fell to $150,000, the insurance company isn't in the red until the investor pulls out six more $25,000 payments—six more years.

The second answer is, the fees are generally between 2% and 4% a year. These premiums are extremely profitable for the insurance companies, especially while withdrawals aren't being made. Many insurance companies also charge the fee on the guaranteed withdrawal amount, which is the one locked in each year if the market rises, not the contract value, which often falls. So in the example above, suppose the contract started at $500,000, stepped up to $625,000, and then fell to $150,000. Here, the 3% might still be charged on $500,000, rather than $150,000. Finally, these premiums and fees are often able to be changed in these products, depending on the differences between the actuarial assumptions and what really happens.

To go back to the eight-year-old analogy: why does the child get a raise in their allowance? Many living benefits on variable annuities offer an annual fixed step-up, even if the markets don't bring the account value up past the previous year's level. In other words, the guaranteed amount goes up 5%, even if the contract value went from $500,000 to $425,000. Therefore, the overarching question for investors pondering these benefits is: Am I willing to pay—handsomely—to know exactly how much money I'll receive every month for the rest of my life, as well as have those payments grow by a predictable amount? If the answer is yes, a variable annuity may be the precise answer. If it's anything else, you probably shouldn't consider one.

To do:

- Check out the Annuity Museum's website. They have the largest collection of annuity memorabilia in the US. http://www. immediateannuities.com/annuitymuseum/

- Reference your retirement planning calculation as referenced above. Look at the gap number. At 5%, what lump sum is needed to fund this annual payment? (Take the gap amount and divide by .05.)
- Ask your planner what living benefits are available to provide you with this income.

Misconception:

Always take the lump sum in a pension plan, not the annuity.

Reality:

Individual circumstances—including cash flow needs, age, health, family & employment situation, tax impact, and other things—all come into play when making this decision.

Proof:

The longer someone is a practitioner of finance, the sooner the realization comes that so many decisions clients make are dependent on a certain trend continuing in the markets—whether it's good or bad. The market rises for a decade and *then* a client wants to get in. Bear markets like 2000-2002 and 2008 happen and *then* clients decide they want to get out and buy bonds.

Unfortunately, decisions are made like this commonly with distributions from corporate retirement plans. A client decides to leave employment—sometimes early, to collect a nice check—and then, taking a quick look at market returns of the past few years, decides that those returns will continue. Then they summarily take the check to their planner, invest it, and begin taking distributions.

And then they wonder what the %&*%^$ happened.

To their credit, many planners now are using the benefits available with variable annuities. Many of these benefits charge higher fees than normal mutual funds or managed accounts, but offer a level sum each year to an investor, regardless of how long they live. If the money in the account runs out, the insurance company will keep paying the income as long as the investor lives.

For those who don't use products like this, the portfolio has to be extremely well-diversified, and even then may be subject to significant systematic risk. Investors also will generally be unable to draw more than 4% of assets a year without depleting principal, according to most studies. Because of this, investors who are inclined towards a very low-fee approach and who aren't concerned about inflation's long-term effect on a fixed sum each month should consider the annuity their company offers.

This may sound strange. After all, it is a nice feeling to know you've got $500,000 or $1MM in your account, and to see the growth on a day-by-day basis. But it works both ways—the "red days" are always twice as bad as the "green days" are good. And you're always wondering: will it still be there? How long do I have, before this money vanishes?

If you're not going to go with a living benefit on a VA, strongly consider the annuity payments offered by your company. They may be smaller, but they are sometimes better than what you could obtain through a comparable private annuity company. Have your planner run some numbers for you. If you're very partial to your planner getting paid, it might be hard for you—typically you can't open an immediate annuity outside your company without being taxed on the whole lump sum as income. Look at the projections your company is providing for you—on payments for your life only and on those to be paid jointly with your spouse. How well do these payments fill any gaps in your existing retirement income? Do they put you "over the top"—that is, having a net retirement income surplus? If so, it's a no-brainer.

If you're convinced you still want to invest and draw principal, make sure you understand the risks involved, especially with the blend of investments you or your planner choose. How have they done historically? How did they fare in 2008? How do they fare with you drawing consistent income on them? All these things can be illustrated for you by a good planner, and should be.

The days of working for forty years at one place and then receiving a healthy pension are long gone, but many employers are still anxious to reward a lifetime of service to their employees. The pension option removes risk for them, since the annuity company is the one on the hook for the payments. Your decision should be based on two things: how much steady retirement income you'll get from going either way, and your comfort level with each path.

To do:

- Take a look at your pension payment from your employer's statement. How does each scenario's payment compare with your retirement income gap, if you have one?
- Have your advisor illustrate a scenario for the lump sum amount you would receive at separation. Ask what the withdrawal rates are, the returns, and the consistency of those returns.
- What are the risks in the second portfolio? Ask your planner what could go wrong.

Misconception:

I'll work until I die. Why do I really need a plan?

Reality:

You need a plan for others, if you refuse to create and implement one for yourself.

Proof:

You generally hear this misconception thinly disguised as a joke. But the reality is that, for a third of those receiving Social Security benefits, these are almost all the retirement income they have. Since there are currently about 58 million people receiving benefits, that means almost 20 million people have no other source of income.

For these people, working may be the only source of additional income they can obtain. SS and SSI benefits were never intended to allow payees to live lavishly. Rather, as Supreme Court Justice Benjamin Cardozo said in a law upholding the constitutionality of the Social Security Act:

"The hope behind this statute is to save men and women from the rigors of the poorhouse, as well as from the haunting fear that such a lot awaits them when journey's end is near."

Very well; the lowest income-earning third of those receiving benefits are likely to remain so. But why not begin a plan—for your heirs, beneficiaries, and family and friends? Many who have never been wealthy intuitively adopt the attitude that fraternity brothers do when they consider hazing: I had to go through it, and so will you. And so they decide, maybe subconsciously: I had to earn it, and so will you.

A nobler approach is possible. If you're still in good health, consider an insurance policy on your own life, even if it's just term. Again, it provides the highest payout possible for the dollars invested, under most conditions. Life insurance contracts are one of the few examples of *aleatory* contracts—contracts that provide a benefit payout much larger than their payin. Many parents save and work and labor all their lives, even foregoing their own retirements so their children can have the things they never did. Yet this same attitude seems to falter when it comes to insurance. Why? Probably because it's never pleasing to consider your own demise.

Other planning techniques are important as well, but for those who don't have a lot of assets, insurance is the easiest way to provide an instant estate. If your health is poor, the best thing you can do is educate your heirs on the value of saving and investing. Jack Canfield, co-author of *Chicken Soup for the Soul*, related a story about a cab driver who asked him how to become a millionaire while driving him to a lecture. Canfield told him to save 10% of his income and invest it. "That's it? No, really. What else do I have to do?" That was it. Easy to hear, but hard to do, for many. Teach your family to pay themselves first—the first creditor on your list of bills to pay is you—ten and twenty and thirty years from now!

To do:

- Sit down, take ten minutes, and think to yourself about your attitude towards money, your whole life. What has your approach been?
- Now think of those you love, and think of the dreams they have, the things they want. Have you helped them to attain them? How?
- If you haven't helped them, decide if you want to. If you want to, talk to your advisor or planner and ask them how you can do so.

Misconception:

My own company's plan is as good as anything else when I retire. Why move the money?

Reality:

There aren't a lot of cases where it makes more sense to leave your money in a retirement plan when you can transfer it to an IRA.

Proof:

There are a number of reasons why retirement plans generally aren't as attractive as IRAs are for investors in retirement. The first one has to do with figuring out what in the world the rules are. In this respect, the Individual Retirement Arrangement (no, the A doesn't stand for account) is generally more estate-friendly than the typical retirement plan. The rules are all in one place for an IRA—check out Publication 590, which is the IRS' governing documents for what you can and can't use them for. With a retirement plan, the governing documents are as varied as the companies themselves. Even if they use IRS prototype plans, the final judgment on the plans rest with the plan sponsors themselves, not the Department of Labor, the IRS, or any other federal agency.

So what does this mean to you? Well, there really are only four periods in an investor's life—four epochs defined by the attitude you take towards your money. Katherine Vessenes, an author, attorney, and financial planner, describes these phases as "BPDT"—Building, Protecting, Distributing, and Transferring your wealth. When you're leaving your job and preparing to retire, you're (hopefully!) done with the "B" and moving into the "P" and "D" categories. In other words, you're done *building* your nest egg; now begins the process of *protecting* it, and nourishing your lifestyle with *distributions* from it.

So far, so good—the main difference between IRAs and your retirement plan at work so far is probably just what investment options there are. But let's look at "T" now—the point at which you decide how your money should be *transferred* to your loved ones. Many retirement plans are distribution-friendly, but few of them are transfer-friendly. Take a husband and wife with several adult children. One spouse is retiring with a plan balance of $700,000, and has enjoyed the client service and relations he's had with his retirement plan. So he decides to keep it there. The client, in this case, has a house owned jointly with his wife worth $400,000, and other accounts worth $350,000. So the total net worth is $1.45 million.

Can you see where this is going? If the spouse designates his wife as primary beneficiary and his children as contingent beneficiaries, and then dies, his wife receives his retirement plan assets of $700,000. She generally won't have to take distributions here; the assets are just hers now. But what would have happened if they had been in an accident simultaneously? Then the children, in all likelihood, would have had to empty the entire account balance over the next one to five years. The entire estate would instantly have been taken as a distribution.

Contrast this with a traditional IRA. Here, the husband could have made the same beneficiary designations, but without his children having to take *en masse* distributions from the account. In other words, the estate, the dynasty, the financial legacy of the client is continued on throughout the entire life expectancies of the heirs—and maybe longer. This is a "stretch" IRA, and it can result in enormous income tax savings over the lifetime of a client.

Many people just think about the investments inside an IRA or a 401(k): "What rate are you getting on your IRA?" "My 401(k) is making 14%!" These are misleading statements—the *investment* inside the account is generating the return, not the account itself! This is what happens when clients think only of one of the four phases of "BPDT." The bottom line: when you're looking at the "B," the extra money contributed on your employer by a match—if you're lucky enough to have one—usually outweighs other investment options. When it comes to the "P" and the "D," you should be having your planner do an analysis of the pros and cons of each strategy—keeping it in your plan vs. rolling it to an IRA. But when the "T" train rolls in to town, the IRA is unmatched for a (simple) generational, tax & estate planning vehicle. Don't miss it!

One final note: There are two areas where it can behoove a client to keep money inside a 401(k) or other retirement plan rather than an IRA: loans and pre-59 1/2 distributions. You will search in vain for an IRA that will permit a loan against it; and you can nearly always access money without the 10% penalty prior to age 59 1/2 at a company you've retired from, provided you leave the money in your plan there.

To do:

- Get a copy of your 401(k) or other retirement plan document.
- Call your company's HR department. Ask for an overview of the investment options.
- Ask your plan sponsor what the distribution options are a) for spousal beneficiaries; and for non-spousal beneficiaries. How do they compare with IRAs, which allow either beneficiary to stretch the account out over their own life expectancies?

Misconception:

I don't mind a lower interest rate as long as I don't lose my principal.

Reality:

Purchasing power risk, not principal risk, is the primary foe of any long-term retirement income initiative.

Proof:

The first job I had was as a bagboy at Great American in upstate New York. I began working there in the fall of 1987, when I was a junior in high school. I would walk the quarter mile downhill from my home for a shift that probably began at 5:00 p.m., then walk back uphill at 9.

I was paid $3.35 per hour. For a moment, let's look at the prices of a few things in 1987.

| One month's rent: $395.00 |
| New car: $10,305.50 |
| Gallon of gas: $.89 |
| Postage stamp: $.24 |
| Dozen eggs: $.65 |

Let's look at them now in 2010.

One month's rent: $780.00
New car: $28,400.00
Gallon of gas: $2.73
Postage stamp: $.44
Dozen eggs: $1.37

The corresponding inflation rate for each of these items is:

Rent: 3.00%
Car: 4.51%
Gas: 4.99%
Stamp: 2.67%
Eggs: 3.29%

Taking an extremely crude "average," we get

3.69%.

This means, simply, that every year you live in retirement (and before it), everything you buy will cost more. Of course, you may use some of these things much more than others. For example, rent might be 30% of your monthly gross income. If that's the case, you can multiply the inflation rate above by a weighting factor of .30. Fuel might be 20% of your income; therefore multiply what you spent on fuel for the month by .20. Doing this will give you a rough idea for what your own PIR—Personal Inflation Rate is.

Of course, most people don't want to do this—you probably have better things to do with your time than figure out what percentage of your pay you spend on microwave popcorn and motor oil. For this reason, financial planners use an assumed inflation rate—typically 3-4%, although it might be as high as 6% for certain types of planning (college costs, for example). If you want to see what the real impact of inflation is, multiply your existing portfolio value by .97 every year—for 30 years. Then see what you get. If you have $1,000,000 saved up at retirement, earning no interest, your remaining sum after the 30 years ends is $401,000—a more than 60% loss. If you're withdrawing money at 4% a year and you earn no interest, the sum drops to $113,000. Simply put: inflation is the greatest long-term enemy of a healthy retirement income.

Now let's go back to our price charts for 1987 and 2010, and add one factor: the price of the Dow Jones Industrial Average.

1987 .INDU—1,938.00

2010 .INDU (9.27.10)—10,812.04

Average annual return: 7.76%

This is over 4% more than our crude inflation rate for the same period. What does this tell you? It tells you that, if you're planning on living off of your assets in retirement, you're going to need equities—dividends and capital appreciation from the greatest businesses in the world. You also should consider real assets, like gold and oil. Want proof? Take a look at the average annual returns of these commodities over the same period, as well as the returns from the Nasdaq (technology) index and the Standard & Poor's 500 index.

Oil—7.08%
Gold—4.77%
.NDX—11.75%
.SPX—6.88%

Does it make sense that, especially in a low interest rate environment, you would want to look at assets whose price cycles don't coincide with bonds and cash? Purchasing power risk, not principal risk, is the true enemy. Paradoxically, as in so many other things in life, the very action we have to take is precisely the one we don't want to—we have to risk some of the *principal* in equities and real assets so we don't lose the entire account's *purchasing power* due to inflation.

By the way, minimum wage—which is what I was paid in 1987—has risen to $8.25—a 4% average annual increase. So for those who resist investing to protect against inflation in their retirement accounts, applying for a part-time job may still be one way to combat inflation. Unfortunately, it may not be the one you want to take. Investing with a consciousness of asset allocation, rebalancing, and a sound understanding of an asset's price cycles is the best way to make sure the money will work when you decide you'd like to stop.

To do:

- Go to http://www.grunderware.com/grunderware/index.htm and take a look at the online Time Value of Money calculator.
- Think about a major purchase you made 20-30 years ago—a car, a home, a large appliance. How much was it? How much does the same model cost today?
- Enter these values into the calculator over the time period so you can calculate the inflation rate on this item. Use the value when you bought it as the present value, the value now as the future value, N for the number of years since you bought, and click on "I". How does the rate compare to the rates above?

Misconception:

I have a retirement plan. I got it from (existing advisor, online, discount firm staff, etc.).

Reality:

To quote Vince Lombardi: "It's not the plan—it's the *execution*."

Proof:

There's a saying that if all the unfilmed movie scripts written in California were ever tossed into the Pacific, drops from the resulting tidal wave would run to the curb of the Bellagio in Las Vegas. Do you call your significant other or friend on Saturday night and ask them if they want to go out and "read a script tonight"? Probably not. Neither should investors smile with pride that "they have a plan." The time to smile is when you have a plan, act according to that plan, and (most likely) have another individual—probably a professional financial advisor—to hold you accountable to that plan. Finally comes the next step—the testing and monitoring of that plan's real-life results with respect to its ability to help you achieve your life goals.

To belabor the metaphor, this really is like the way movies are made. I like to tell clients that they are the stars; the planner is the director. (This is a fluid relationship; it's hard to imagine that J. Lo's word wouldn't outweigh a less well-known director, or that the starlet of the month would be able to impose her will on James Cameron.) Even further, the vision—the story—really belongs to the client. Isn't that what we go to the screen to see?

Every financial planning process has at least four steps. The first is the vision; the client's definition of what they want to achieve. It may be coerced out of them in a passive sense, under probing from a good planner. More enduring goals—and ideal clients for most planners—emerge from those clients who have a vision, a burning desire, an active motivation to succeed and flourish financially. This is a 29-year-old Sylvester Stallone dreaming of a movie about a nobody giving the heavyweight champ a run for his money, watching Muhammad Ali knocked out by an unknown fighter on TV a few days later, and writing one of the greatest stories of all time in three days. Then starring in it! Your plan may not be as ambitious as Stallone's—you may merely want to know how much you need to retire comfortably, or learn how to manage different kinds of risks in your financial life. Regardless, that vision—that dream of how it could be, how you want it to be—this is the first step.

The second step is the script—in financial terms, the plan. There's a saying in Hollywood: "If it ain't on the page, it ain't on the stage." In the movie business, the script has to make you laugh or cry. In the financial planning business, the plan has to do one thing—provide a clear set of directions towards an investor's dreams.

Third comes the filming. Casting calls are made, talent is recruited, budgets and wardrobe, sound effects, lights and camera crews, food and beverage, makeup and the other dozens of key movie people get together, rehearse and act out the scenes, and create the reels. This is where everybody sweats. Acting is hard work—so hard that, paraphrasing Michael Shurtleff, discoverer of Dustin Hoffman and Barbra Streisand:

"Acting is really only for a certain kind of person. If you think you might want to be an actor, but you could do something else—do something else."

It's no different with financial planning. Having recommendations, asset allocation and rebalancing decisions, and procedures is one thing. Sticking to them in bull and bear markets is another. This is 75%+ of the reason you pay a financial advisor—to help you manage your emotions, so your emotions don't manage your behavior. If you're not telling your mind what to think, it will think for you! And, very typically, it won't get farther than the market fluctuations of the day. Instead, why not employ a planner who can help you filter those thoughts through the prism of history—a history in which equities have outpaced fixed income investments by a factor of 2 to 1 in real returns, and 3 to 1 in nominal returns?

And then comes the fourth stage—the edit. The post-production group gets together and cuts the scene where Sandra Bullock was talking with salad greens in her teeth, or where the fat extra in the back waved to the camera. The final product has ADRs, Foleys, special effects, musical scores, lighting changes added in. The final product is (hopefully) beautiful enough to make the audience cry. Most importantly, the vision of the original storyteller is accomplished. What was only a vision in the writer's mind has now jumped alive, a living, breathing being that the world is watching.

This is akin to the monitoring stage in financial planning, but, over longer periods, it can also connote the reward of a job well done at certain milestones—retirement, a graduation from college, marriage or the purchase of a dream home. Most commonly, it corresponds to the annual review—the time when planner and client meet to examine how well the "production" is coming along.

Keep one thing in mind, when going through all these stages: the client is always the star! Many actors are notoriously shy people, and getting in front of the camera makes them unusually vulnerable. Perhaps nowhere else in business is this vulnerability so similar as in financial planning. It seems a reasonable assertion that this shyness is in direct proportion to the potential reward. Acting out your plan may not get you anywhere near next year's Oscars, but it will get you to where you want to be financially.

To do:

- Take a look at your financial plan. Look at your notes. When was the last time you reviewed it—either alone or with another?
- What's your vision? Take all the stops out; forget about money for a minute. If someone dropped you on a desert island, and there was only one activity you could pursue, what would it be? How does that information fit into your plan?
- What do you need to change? Call your planner or someone you trust and revise your plan, introducing those changes.

Misconception:

I've done my plan. Isn't that enough?

Reality:

This is another version of the same tune we heard before. Again: it's not enough to create a plan, or even enough to follow a plan. You have to review the plan—in the light of your own goals as well as what markets will actually give you—and make sure that it actually works.

Proof:

Secular markets often create trends in planning that are unrealistic. (By secular, I mean a market that has one prevailing trend—whether up, down, or flat—for a long period of time, typically years and even decades.) For example, I have a client who had a previous advisor tell him he would easily be able to withdraw 10-12% a year from his retirement account—without running out of money. Those words were quite true—if history continued unabated forever in a perfect replica of 1982-1999.

It didn't.

Mark Twain said: "Never try to walk across a river whose average depth is four feet." The same is true of making retirement income predictions based off of steady, unvarying returns without a) accounting for inflation; and b) going back very far historically to avoid a biased picture of asset returns. Doing this is very dangerous—for client and advisor.

Suppose, for example, that you had a $250,000 portfolio, and planned to take 5% withdrawals every year on it to augment your other income. According to the results of a case study assembled by Prudential Financial, the sequence of the returns—the order in which they were received—is more important when taking distributions out than when they're left alone. In fact, if two assets experience the same returns year-by-year, but simply in a different sequence, the amount of money left at the end is the same—provided nothing was withdrawn.

Let's look at this closer. The investor mentioned above invests her $250,000 into a portfolio of stocks and funds, and experiences the following returns over the next 10 years:

6.7%
16.9%
7.1%
-3.0%
15.4%
8.3%
6.4%
-3.5%
-12.8%
-17.6%

At the end of the period, she has

$298,694

Remaining. If we reverse the order, so that the returns look like

-17.6%
-12.8%
-3.5%
6.4%
8.3%
15.4%
-3.0%
7.1%

JOEL T. REDMOND, CFP ®

16.9%
6.7%

And we get

$298,694—a perfect match. But what happens when we pull money out—say 5% of the original amount each year? If this happens, the first scenario above looks like this:

$253,412
$281,626
$288,234
$267,462
$294,226
$305,109
$311,336
$288,377
$240,564
$187,925

The investor has less than they started with, but at least there's more than 70% of the original value left. But now look at what happens if the investor's returns are reversed and they're taking money out, as so often happens when people retire in bear markets:

$195,700
$159,750
$142,096
$137,890
$135,798
$142,286
$125,892
$121,443
$127,354
$122,550

In this case, the investor has less than half her money left. The first plan works a great deal better than the second; most investors want to live off as much interest income as they can. Clearly, it's better to experience bull markets first, then bear markets later, when you're taking retirement money. Many plans don't address this at all; fewer still aggressively plan around it. It isn't hard to see the accompanying agita here. "I picked the wrong time to retire."

This is a fallacy. The time to retire shouldn't depend on what the world economy is doing; it should depend on your own life, health, and family situation! The answer isn't to agonize over what can't be controlled—world asset prices. Instead, investors need to focus on what they can control—their response to these events, in the form of a sound plan that addresses the risks they bring to their savings.

To do:

- Ask your planner what average annual returns they're using in your own retirement planning calculations. If you haven't had them do one, ask them to!
- Ask what steps you should take to manage sequence of return risk in your portfolio, and if it's something you need to be concerned about.
- Check out this brief paper from Karp Capital Management, which addresses this type of risk. http://www.karpcapital.com/downloads/Sequence-Clicks.pdf

Misconception:

It'll all be gone and I don't even want to look at it. Why bother?

Reality:

You can use this excuse for any type of productive behavior. Whether anything is left or not, looking at a less-than-desirable retirement income situation straight in the eye is better than avoiding it.

Proof:

"Why should we kill these murderers? They'll only kill again." "Why should I cut my fingernails? They'll just grow long again." So went the interchange between the Mossad agent Avner and his case officer Ephraim, characters in Steven Spielberg's 2004 classic *Munich*. The same argument applies when this misconception is voiced, and you start hearing it in prolonged bear markets. The monthly statements mount and mount, unopened on the desk—or shunted into the recycling. The gnawing feeling exists in the back of your mind, nameless, shapeless, but still there. You know there isn't enough—all you remember is hearing your friends talk about their investment decisions, and they seem so out of your league. One by one, they go off to Boca, to Phoenix, even to the south of France. You'll never get there, it seems.

Or will you? In the spring of 2010, after a series of workshops I'd conducted on Social Security, a very sweet, conscientious attendee agreed afterward to come in for a visit. We looked—hard—at her resources for income in retirement, and her outlook was very glum indeed—at least, from talking to her. We performed a retirement planning estimate for the amount she would need to save, using conservative, hard-boiled numbers for her life expectancy, desired income, tax bracket, rates of return and inflation, and retirement age. Then we looked at her resources, and we found out that she wasn't quite so bad off as she thought. In fact, I told her, she would be able to retire comfortably at age 66 with a significant surplus in her retirement savings.

Tears welled up in this client's eyes. "Are you sure?" she asked me. I told her I was; I had had the numbers checked several times. Then I did them again, right in front of her. She continued, saying that all her working life, she had never felt like she was one of the "in" crowd when it came to investing. Consequently, she felt like her own prospects for retirement were bleak. Now, I assured her, she could take comfort knowing that a significant obstacle to her retirement happiness was removed—the portrait of austerity she had painted for herself in her own mind, supplied by the canvas and colors of not knowing how to translate what she had accumulated into what it could pay her, and for how long.

In this case, the client's not looking at her assets and investments over the years paid off in one extremely happy moment—when she found out how good the news was. But, I wonder, how many years had she spent wondering, even agonizing over whether or not she would be able to support herself post-full time work? The investment performance is enough reason for any client to look sooner, rather than later, at the portfolio. But a more important reason—the most important reason—is the emotional payoff. You should "bother" to look at your retirement plan often—and, if you aren't sure how to read it, hire someone who will. The emotional payoff that often results between now and your retirement "D-Day" can be immeasurable.

To do:

- Ask yourself—with no one else around—how you really feel about the prospect of living off of your assets in retirement. What's your reaction?
- Think about the same thing, at the same time, into a tape recorder.
- Listen to the tape recorder. What are you hearing?

Misconception:

I DON'T NEED an estate plan.

Reality:

You already *have* an estate plan, whether you realize it or not. The question to be asked is: who will be paid more, your loved ones or the government?

Proof:

There are only a few ways property passes from one person to another when one of them dies—by trust, by contract, or by operation of law. The two latter ones are often entered into many years before the decedent's passing, sometimes without a thought of what happens at that time.

Property transfers at death by *contract* are your IRA, retirement plans, and life insurance policies. The retirement assets or death benefit proceeds don't pass through probate; they simply pass directly to whoever you listed on your beneficiary designation statement. In plainer English, this means you can't include these types of accounts in your will—they're going to go to whoever is designated as your beneficiary in the contract.

The third type of property transfer occurs naturally when property is titled jointly between spouses. This type of joint ownership, called joint tenancy with right of survivorship, automatically gives one spouse a 50% interest in any property so titled, however it was obtained in the first place. This is property transfer by *operation of law.* So this means when one spouse dies, the other automatically becomes 100% sole owner of the property, without any need for legal proceedings. For that reason—probate avoidance—JTWROS can be very useful. The problem with it begins to occur as the owners become wealthier. Why? Well, the main reason is that the decedent's 50% interest is included in his gross estate. This doesn't create a problem at the death of the first spouse, but can often result in estate tax being due at the death of the second.

Interestingly enough, the IRS—with that same paternal concern that so many of us have—has created a massive insurance policy for their own loved ones. (The loved ones are, of course, themselves.) All right, I'm being tongue in cheek. But this is all the estate tax is. In the same way that your beneficiary receives an insurance check when you die, Uncle Sam receives a very large check when anyone (with a qualifier) dies. The qualifiers, beginning in 2011, are: they have to have a taxable estate over $5 million. "Well, no worries—I'm not there," many say. That's fine, but the exemption has been as low as $1 million in the past ten years. If it reverts there in 2013 (the $5MM amount holds until then), many will be caught unawares. Many people aren't as far away from this as they thought. For example, a widow still living in her own home worth $500,000, with no real debt, and with retirement accounts and an annuity or two worth $550,000 will qualify. While these sums are well above the average home values and retirement plan assets in the US, they obviously aren't tokens of the filthy rich.

So what happens in this case? Well, if the widow dies, she will have to pay a federal estate tax on the $50,000 in excess of the $1,000,000. This tax is assessed at 55%. Yes, fifty-five percent. And that's just the federal estate tax; there are also state estate taxes. So, if we only count the federal tax, this widow's beneficiaries will pay $27,500 in taxes on her estate.

You don't have to do very much work to see how punitive this can get for the rich—and how lucrative for the IRS. The same widow in the same situation with twice the values—$1,000,000 for the house and $1,100,000 for the accounts—would pay 55% of the amount over $1,000,000, or 55% of $1,100,000. This amounts to $605,000!

Finally, another sinister consequence arises when most of the wealth is tied up in retirement accounts: income tax due on money taken out to pay estate tax. I can hear you saying "huh?" in the background. Well, say that the whole estate was in one IRA worth $2,100,000. The same tax is due as in the other instance—$605,000. But now, let's assume the heirs don't have that sitting in checking to just pay at the time the tax is due—usually a pretty valid assumption. If this is the case, you have to pull the money out of the IRA itself. But if you need $605,000, and the tax bracket of the beneficiaries is 25%, you need to pull out $806,667. That's another $200,000 lost immediately to the government for income taxes, just to pay the estate taxes!

This is where certain types of trusts can be enormously beneficial for wealthy people. For example, in the last case, the family could have purchased a life insurance policy on the widow, and placed it in a special trust where, on her death, the check would be made available to pay some of these taxes without having to tap the IRA. The tax savings in these types of situations can be massive. In general, trusts are created to do one of five things—avoid probate, allow for professional money or asset management, shelter money from taxes, allow control over the disposition of wealth, and protect assets (usually for access to entitlement programs like Medicaid). The irony is that the IRA has already written up an enormous contract, with the terms inevitably in their favor when dealing with a wealthy person. This contract makes them the potential beneficiary of more than half of the wealth of the richest people in the country.

So, back to the original question: do you need an estate plan? No, if you don't care how much of your wealth the IRS gets. No, if you aren't ever going to have your assets cross the $5,000,000 threshold. And no, if you're perfectly content with your heirs possibly waiting six to eighteen months to receive the physical parts of your legacy, if they aren't disinherited because of a fact you didn't know about and didn't have an attorney check for you.

To do:

- Assess what your net worth is right now—assets minus liabilities. Use the statement of financial position referenced in the first section of this book. What is it?
- Compound this value at 8% from now until your life expectancy—say an average is 81 for men and 84 for women. Use the online calculator from the last section. http://www.grunderware.com/grunderware/index.htm

- Is the sum over $1MM? If so, you need an estate plan. Talk to your attorney. (Even if it's close but not quite there, you may want to create a plan anyway.)

Misconception:

I'll leave it all to my spouse.

Reality:

Leaving everything to a surviving spouse, while freeing them from paying any estate tax on the death of the first spouse, often results in a great deal more estate tax due at the surviving spouse's death; and the wealthier each spouse is, the more dangerous the estate tax situation becomes.

Proof:

Let's talk about Anne for a moment. Anne is 84 years old. She drives her own car wherever she wants, doesn't eat a grain of sugar or caffeine, and is always asked "are these your sisters?" whenever she goes anywhere with her daughters. She is also a widow; her husband predeceased her in 2006.

Now we'll talk about her assets. She lives in a lovely home that her late husband built for her in Central New York, assessed at $2 million. She also possesses retirement accounts—his TIAA-CREF plan from his days as a university professor—amounting to a little more than that, about $2.75 million. Her summer cottage on Block Island is worth a little more, about $2.3 million. She also has bank accounts and a few insurance policies with cash value, perhaps $50,000 worth. Finally, she has some artwork and automobiles and personal effects; we'll say these are worth $150,000. So, in total, we have:

$2 million—home
$2.75 million—TIAA-CREF
$2.3 million—cottage on Block Island
$50,000—bank accounts
$150,000—personal effects
$7,350,000—total estate

Now let's talk about her estate. She's in perfect health, so it's very reasonable she could live another 10 or 15 years. But what if she died in 2011? What would happen to her heirs as they inherited the assets? Well, looking at the federal estate tax, we can see from the last section that they would owe 35% of the amount over $5,000,000, which means 35% of $2,350,000. This means $822,500 of tax is due. Where will it come from? Well, the house could be sold to liquidate the debt. Suppose, however, that the house was left to one of the children, who refused to sell. OK, what about the cottage? Same situation—one of the daughters simply couldn't imagine living without a getaway. She won't sell. OK, so we have to liquidate the accounts. (The personal effects will probably take too long to sell.) Well, that takes care of $150,000 of the tax. Where does the other $772,500 come from?

You guessed it—the retirement account would have to be tapped to pay the tax. If this is the case, that means the TIAA-CREF account, at the 25% bracket, would have to give up over $1 million—more than a third of the account! The value of the estate is now

$7,350,000 - ($772,500 / 1.25) = $7,350,000 - $1,030,000 = $6,320,000

The estate has shrunk by 14%—about one-seventh of the original amount. Ouch!

So how could this have been avoided? The simplest way would have been for her late husband to leave a portion of the TIAA-CREF assets to one or more of the children. How much should he have left to them? Enough so that her estate would grow to no more than (ideally) $5 million by the end of her life, at a minimum. At a maximum, his entire unified credit amount! If he had done this, neither he or she would have paid a dime of estate tax—a savings of over $1 million! So if he had gone to a planner and attorney and had some numbers crunched, he could have realized a savings of $1 million—for a few hours' consultations that may have run him $5,000. Not a bad trade.

"But that was 5 years earlier!" I hear you saying. "How could he know where the rates were going?" He could have known by hiring a planner. Even if he couldn't have done this, a telephone call to the attorney asking about potential estate issues would have been enough to start the process rolling.

OK. We looked at the case when my friend died young. What if she lives to be 99, and the TIAA-CREF assets and the house are growing at 7%? In that case, we'll have:

$7,587,000	TIAA-CREF
$5,518,000	House
$6,345,000	Cottage
$50,000	Accounts
$413,000	Personal effects
$19,913,000	Total value of estate

Here we have a genuine problem. If matters are left alone and no trusts or special arrangements have been made, estate tax of over $5.2 *million* will be levied on this estate. Make no mistake: if the house can't be sold to cover this, the TIAA-CREF account will be almost totally wiped out. Why? Because, again: at the 25% tax bracket, you have to pull out over $6.93 *million* to arrive at the amount of estate tax due. Bye-bye love, bye-bye happiness—and bye-bye retirement! Keep in mind that not only does all this money vanish into the amorphous, faceless mists of the IRS, but it does so at the *worst* possible time—when you're mourning the loss of your loved one. The feelings of loneliness and memory are compounded by the resentment anyone would feel that the government took nearly all the retirement money—simply by default!

"So when *can* I leave it to my spouse?" I hear you saying. In general, you can leave your entire estate to your spouse if you a) have less than the applicable exemption amount (the amount that passes free of estate tax) of $5 million (in 2011-12); b) have no children, grandchildren, or younger heirs that you want to leave the money to; or c) want the government to collect half or more of your money. Really, a) is the most likely scenario. If you're in any other one—talk to a planner or an attorney!

To do:

- Take a crude inventory of your "stuff." This includes what's on your statement of financial position, your personal assets, and any business interests.

- Is the value over $5,000,000? If so, talk to your attorney and ask what avenues you can look at regarding planning around the estate tax.
- If the value's under $5,000,000, figure out what it might be worth when you die. Choose a conservative life expectancy—say 81 for women, 84 for men—and a growth rate, maybe 7-8% per annum. Then figure out what it will be worth at your decease. Is it over $1 million now? http://www.grunderware.com/grunderware/index.htm

Misconception:

We have everything titled jointly.

Reality:

Titling everything jointly (especially when all other non-probate assets are left directly to a surviving spouse) at its worst is equivalent to flushing $1,750,000 down the toilet.

Proof:

The unified transfer tax system discussed a few sections ago provides for one escape route from estate tax being due at the second spouse's death, in most cases: the *unified credit*. Basically, this credit is a dollar-for-dollar reduction in actual estate tax due at the death of a decedent. (Keep in mind this section currently only applies to decedents with $5 million or more of assets in their estate.) It works like this: you find the actual amount of estate tax due, then apply the credit against it.

So why is it a waste to use the unified credit with a spousal beneficiary? The answer is the marital deduction that decedents receive when leaving assets to a surviving spouse. This deduction is *unlimited* in amount.

Let's take a successful couple, Sam and Heather. They have $11MM of assets—some left to them by inheritance and some by savings and successful investing through retirement accounts.

Sam and Heather want to make sure that they're doing everything right for their estate plan. Sam is ten years older than Heather, so he plans to leave her everything at his death. What happens? Well, if we assume $7 million is titled in Sam's name, and $4 million in Heather's name, Sam decides to leave everything to his wife when he dies, even though he has three adult kids of his own from a previous marriage.

Sam passes away. The $7 million goes directly to Heather, and she pays no estate tax on it. She grieves and moves on. Ten years later, her assets have grown to $15 million. She dies, and leaves the assets to her single middle-aged daughter Kim.

Still sorrowing, Kim gets a bill from the US government for the tax due upon settling of the estate. Her heart skips a beat when she reads the paper, then she laughs to herself and assumes it must be a mistake. *$3.5 million? Something's not right here. I thought Mom said she had an estate plan,* Kim says to herself.

Calling the attorney, Kim finds out things are worse than she thought, not better. Because all of Mom's assets were qualified (i.e. in IRA and other tax-deferred accounts), she has to pull out additional money to pay the tax bill. Kim is in the 28% tax bracket, so she has to pull out $3,500,000 / (1 - .28) = $4.861 million. Almost a third of the estate is now gone.

Why? Because Sam didn't use the government's freebie for him—the unified credit. In 2011 and 2012, the federal government allows estates a credit against their tax bills in the amount of the tax that normally would be levied against the first $5 million of that estate. Since the federal estate tax rate is 35%, this amounts to $1.75 million. If Sam had simply left the first $5 million to his kids instead of Heather, Heather would have received $2 million free of estate tax, and Sam's kids would have gotten $5 million free of estate tax. If Heather's estate then grew to, say, $9 million at her death, she would have only had $4 million that would have been taxable to Kim, because the first $5 million would have been covered under *her* unified credit. So Kim would have still gotten a big tax bill—it would have been $1.4 million, which means she would have had to raid the IRAs for $1.94 million—but at least that's only 21.5% of the estate, not 32%.

So how does titling stuff jointly enter into this? Well, when you title assets jointly (at least, between husband and wife under JTWROS, or joint tenancy with right of survivorship), you miss out on the freebie described above—the *unified credit*. Even though you as the first spouse to die might not be there to see the $1.75 million lost to Uncle Sam, your surviving spouse will. At the worst possible time—when they're emotionally distraught with your passing.

So how can you avoid this? Talk to your attorney. If your estate is under $5 million and you don't expect it to grow there, don't bother. But if you have a sneaking suspicion that you might get there, make an appointment. This credit has changed a great deal in the past ten years—it's ranged from its current high of $1.75 million (through 1.1.2013) and was as low as $345,800 (2002-2003). Don't speed to WalMart for a "buy one/get one" and neglect the biggest coupon most American taxpayers can get!

To do:

- Ask your attorney to give you a rough idea of what your estate tax would be if you passed away today. Then ask if that accounts for the full use of your unified credit.
- Ask your CPA or planner the same thing.
- Take a look at IRS Form 1041, as well as the instructions for it. You can find it here: http://www.irs.gov/pub/irs-pdf/f1041.pdf

Misconception:

I don't want to think about dying.

Reality:

Refusing to make plans for fear of dying is as illogical as refusing to buy auto insurance for fear of crashing. In fact, it's much more illogical, because of the absolute certainty of death, as opposed to the questionable certainty of a car accident.

Proof:

Do you remember the last scenes of the movie *Titanic,* just before the boat went into the water? The quartet played *Orpheus* for the scrambling passengers and tight-jawed pursers, trying to keep order on the ship. John

Jacob Astor, Benjamin Ingersoll, and the other first class passengers strolled down to the ballroom in their finest outfits, whistling for brandy and saying they were prepared to go down "like gentlemen." As the boat tilted waterward, a priest read passages from the Bible to a small band of faithful, while the rank and file of passengers frantically made their way to the rear of the vessel, hundreds of feet above the water now.

Why bring this up? Well, you're on the *Titanic*, and so am I, and so is everyone you know. The only difference between us, at our various stages of life, is whether we know we've hit the iceberg yet. The ones who know first—what do they do? They get near the lifeboats.

Estate planning is like this. It doesn't save your life—trusts and wills aren't wonder drugs and they don't raise anyone from the dead. But facing facts and developing an estate plan can save the livelihood of your family, your legacy, and your future—sooner rather than later.

It seems like such a basic message, right? But there's strong evidence that it isn't being followed. According to a survey done by CFP Board in 2009, only 38% of respondents with assets of $1 million or more have a financial plan in place and have it regularly updated. Thirty-eight percent—and this is millionaires and up only! Truly, the IRS must be licking their lips—because a roaring flood of estate tax revenue is coming their way. If the AEA (we talked about this in the past few sections) reverts to $1 million in 2013, many of these people may be vulnerable to this tax. Another 35% of these people have never had a financial plan at all! (The other 27% have had a plan at some time but haven't had it updated.)

Of the 2,223 passengers on board the *Titanic*, 711 survived. This translates to 31.76%, or less than one-third. Compared to the number of millionaires who have a regularly updated plan, the truth is slightly encouraging—it seems like more of these people are getting near the lifeboats. But among those whose assets are between $100,000 and $1 million, the number falls to 30%; combined regardless of asset level, it drops to 17%.

The bottom line is something you already knew: ignoring the problem won't make it go away. Newsflash for you: we're all on the same ship—and it's hit an iceberg. Get near a lifeboat! Have your estate plan examined today.

To do:

- Call a friend you trust, a planner, or your attorney and ask them to walk you through what actually happens when you die. In other words, ask about the proverbial "friend" with similar assets, liabilities, and familial situation as yours.
- Ask your attorney where the best place is to store your most critical documents—the ones that your heirs would need if you were to pass suddenly.
- Put them there!

Misconception:

My kids can't handle the money. Leave them out.

Reality:

There are numerous estate planning vehicles—often specific types of trusts—that are explicitly designed to manage any behavioral traits in your heirs that might damage the legacy you leave them.

Proof:

Thomas Paine said, "That which we obtain too easily, we esteem too lightly." We see evidence of this every day—according to the Consumerist blog, 1 in 3 lottery winners are broke within 5 years. Some private studies place this estimate even higher—according to the Journal Star, a Connecticut newspaper, one team of financial advisors places the amount of lottery winners to go broke at 70%. "We know from studies and our own internal research that when new wealth is created in a family, there is a 90% probability that all of that wealth will be gone by the third generation," said Darl LePage of Brook Wealth Management in Rocky Hill, CT. "And that's among families who have worked hard for years to achieve success. When people receive sudden wealth, like in a lottery jackpot, the numbers are much worse."

The problem isn't that these tendencies exist—the problem is thinking there's nothing to do about them. One potential approach can work well with the proverbial "diamonds in the rough"—those children, grandchildren, or other loved ones who you know have their hearts in the right place but haven't had success managing money. The tool here might be a Section 2503(b) trust, also called the "Bad Boy's Trust."

A Section 2503 (b) trust is a vehicle that allows the one who creates it—called the *grantor*—to divide the gift to the (usually minor) child into two parts—an annual income amount and a principal (also called *corpus*) amount. Under the terms of the trust, it's not possible to avoid giving the beneficiary something prior to reaching a more mature age—income must be distributed at least annually. But the corpus, which contains the majority of the value of the trust, doesn't need to be distributed to the child until age 21, or even higher. Typically, this can be delayed until the completion of a specific goal, such as college or graduate school—even a set number of years afterward.

A second type of trust exists that has similarities to the Section 2503 (b) trust. This type of trust is simply called a "pour-over" trust—it's a revocable living trust that becomes irrevocable at the grantor's death. Typically, it's used to allow the grantor to designate assets to be given to loved ones, but not until he or she is judged incapable of making decisions for himself, or dies, at which point the trust becomes irrevocable. Essentially, this allows the grantor to keep "strings" for a specific period of time—usually until death or cognitive impairment (at which time a designated trustee takes over to ensure the beneficiary receives his portion of the interest).

Finally, many trusts have "spendthrift" provisions in them, which typically protect the assets of the trust from beneficiaries' creditors until they actually assume possession of them. Other provisions of this type are similar to the 2503 (b) trust in that they will postpone an unruly or irresponsible heir's inheritance until a specific age, or perhaps in stages. For example, the total inheritance might be divided into thirds, with each third being distributed at a specified age.

As a final thought, it might be beneficial for donors to realize that there's a point at which even the most immature child reaches an age of accountability. These various types of estate tools enable grantors to postpone their generosity, without disinheriting their loved ones—in some cases a valuable lesson to the heirs. But to exclude loved ones altogether leaves charity, or the Treasury—perhaps too hard a lesson for any disinherited loved one to learn.

To do:

- Talk to your attorney and ask what arrangements exist to grant you a degree of control over your distribution of assets. Do you need such control?
- Make sure to ask what the disadvantages are of these arrangements, including cost, loopholes, ease of administration, etc.
- Take the information to someone else you trust, either another attorney, or perhaps someone who specializes in estate law. What are their thoughts?

Misconception:

My kids are well off. I don't need a plan.

Reality:

Depending on what you plan to do with the money that might have gone to your kids, you may end up paying just as much or more in taxes as if you'd left it to them outright.

Proof:

(DISCLAIMER: The arguments below are valid ONLY if the AEA (applicable exemption amount) reverts to the 2001 level of $1 million. Note that the year used is 2013, NOT the years 2011-2012. The scenario below is NOT valid for tax years 2011-2012, because this amount has been raised to $5 million. A more conservative scenario is shown below, to illustrate what *could* happen again in 2013.)

There are three taxes in the unified transfer tax system talked about, above. The first two are the federal gift and estate taxes. The third is a much less well-known tax called the *generation—skipping transfer tax (GSTT)*. This tax was designed almost a century ago to ensure that enormously wealthy families wouldn't be able to avert taxes on the transfer of their money by "skipping" a generation—i.e. giving it to their grandchildren instead of their children.

Let's look at an example. Suppose (assume this is 2013 and the 2001 estate tax levels apply) you've got a $10 million estate, and you're thinking about ways you can "share the wealth" before you get any older. Your kids are great; all of them are financially self-sufficient. But your grandson Bobby is a computer programming prodigy and has already produced six patents for Microsoft. Now he wants to create his own startup and has talked more than once about going public. What's more, he's nineteen! You firmly resolve: all right, this kid's gotta get *something*. You give him $4 million.

So far, so good. Because you read a lot, you already know that the gift itself isn't anything you'll have to pay taxes on—your heirs are the ones that'll deal with that. But one day in your study, you come across an article (maybe this one!) on the GSTT and your knees buckle. "What have I done?" you say. You go clean your reading glasses, because you just read in print that the GSTT is assessed *in addition* to any gift tax that will be payable at death to settle your estate. You get your pen out and do some rough calculations:

Gift: $4 million
Annual exclusion amount: $10,000
Taxable gift: $3.99 million

Now you remember that there's an applicable exemption amount for the GSTT, just like there is for the estate and gift taxes. It's $1 million. So, using the formula the IRS gives us, we get

$1 million/$4 million to get something we call an *applicable fraction*—this is the first number we use in figuring out what the GSTT's actually going to be. Taking

1—applicable fraction (.25) =

.75, which is what we call the *inclusion ratio*. This number, multiplied by the highest estate tax bracket (55%), is the actual effective tax rate the GSTT is going to come in at on the transfer. It works out to:

(.75) (.55) ($3.99 million) = $1.65 million

This is 41% of the gift—but we're not even done! Now you have to figure out what the *gift* tax would be. Sparing the calculations and using 2011 values for everything, we get

$1.85 million

Adding these two sums gives us:

$3.5 million—87.5% of the entire gift!

Bewildered, you sit down and wonder how on earth you're going to be able to share this bad news with your children—that the $4 million wasn't a gift to Bobby from you, but a gift to the government from them! Unable to focus, your head still swimming from these numbers, you crunch them again—and again. Still the same. Too ashamed to speak, you resolve to do your best to make it up to them—but you're not going to tell them. Not yet, anyway.

Fast forward two years. A tearful couple stand before the priest on a cold day in the spring, listening to the eulogy. Bobby's standing right with them, tears rolling down his eyes. The couple walks slowly away and drives back home. Later that week, still numb with grief, the couple recoil in shock when the attorney tells them they owe $5 million in estate, gift and generation-skipping transfer tax. To get the money for it, they need to liquidate $6 million of assets.

In the old Westerns, and in almost any action movie, even the bad guys won't usually cut up a man after a gunfight once he's fallen—you don't kick a man when he's down, the saying goes.

The IRS does, though.

Call your planner, attorney, or other advisor and make sure you—or worse, your family—won't get kicked when you're down.

To do:

- Talk with your estate attorney and ask them to explain the mechanics of the GSTT. Can you think of anyone you know that might have to pay this tax? Do you?
- If the answer is yes, ask the attorney to give you some ideas of how to mitigate the effects of the tax.
- Ask the attorney to run scenarios of the different methods suggested—trusts, charitable donations, and life insurance all come to mind. Can any of these help you? How?

Misconception:

I have a revocable living trust.

Reality:

The revocable living trust, while often a very useful tool for removing assets from the probate process, is useless for removing assets from a decedent's estate.

Proof:

As mentioned above, there are five general reasons to use a trust. The first reason is to remove assets from the probate estate—essentially, to ensure that the decedent is able to share the wealth with the heirs privately, and in a timely manner. The second is tax savings—to remove a part of the decedent's assets from the estate tax. Next comes management; many trusts are established because of the money management capabilities of a specific institution. Fourth is flexibility—the ability to select which beneficiaries receive what assets, limiting some and allowing others to receive part of the wealth. Finally, trusts are often created to provide asset protection—essentially, to ensure that someone's wealth isn't seized by the government due to eligibility for entitlements like Medicaid.

Revocable living trusts are essentially formed for two reasons: to avoid probate and to take advantage of a capable trust manager. To be most effective, they must be fully funded—i.e. you'll only be able to keep assets out of probate if you actually put them in the trust. They also can be useful in the event of incapacity or incompetency—that is, if someone is found medically unfit to govern his or her own affairs.

A comment on the first reason may be causing some to ask what probate is. An article from New York Life defines it well:

"Probate is a court proceeding. It is the legal process by which a person's final debts are settled and legal title to property is formally passed from the decedent to his or her beneficiaries and heirs."

There are three steps to probate: the inventory of probate assets, settling the decedent's debts, and transferring the property. The main reason you would want to avoid this—especially if you have a large estate—is the complexity, the cost, the delay, and the lack of privacy—probate documents are public record once filed.

The problem for many who establish these vehicles occurs when they forget to fund the trusts. The trust can only remove assets from the probate process if the assets are put into them. This is called "funding" a trust and consists of transferring all assets held in the grantor of the trust's separate title, and re-titling it in the name of the trustee of the trust. If this isn't done, the trust won't remove the assets from probate, which can take eighteen months or more, depending on the area.

A further complication arises with the second aim of these trusts: the incapacity of the grantor once the trust is established but not yet funded. If there's no provision in the trust document naming a successor trustee—usually a child or grandchild—the entire purpose of the trust is defeated. Those considering their own future incapacity, cognitive disorder, or other life-altering impairment will typically put in a provision allowing for two doctors to confirm the grantor's incapacity before the successor trustee can take over the grantor's financial affairs. Once this is done, the trust can be funded even after the grantor's incapacity—the successor trustee can fund it, ensuring the assets will be shielded from the often-lengthy and inconvenient probate process.

Finally: revocable living trusts don't remove anything from a grantor's estate for tax purposes. I always consider it an unenviable task when I've had to tell a client or prospective client that their heirs will still be responsible for any estate tax due when they pass. The look I've gotten in one or two cases makes me wonder if the attorney told them they were getting a trust, or a magical talisman of some sort! "Sign here and we'll take away the taxes—and you'll have new superpowers to combat evil!" The clue is the word *revocable*—the fact that you can revoke something means you haven't given up your rights to it. Only *irrevocable* trusts can do that—and shield any of your assets (again, over the exemption) from estate tax. Estate planning is complicated! The government is unusually clever when it comes to generating tax revenue from rich people—especially when they die. Make sure you fully understand what any trusts you have are designed to do, and then check with your EP team to make sure they're actually doing it.

To do:

- Dig out any trust documents you have and scan them for a moment. Do you have any trust established? Are they revocable or irrevocable?
- Consider these five objectives for any trust work: tax savings, asset protection, flexibility in selecting beneficiaries, avoiding probate, and management expertise. Which is most important to you? (It can be more than one, but prioritize them.)
- Share these objectives with your attorney and ask if any trusts you have help you meet these objectives. Ask how they do this. Is there anything else that should be added to your estate plan?

Misconception:

I'll gift later on, just before I go.

Reality:

The more money you have, the more estate tax your heirs may have to pay, unless you establish a systematic program of gifting throughout your lifetime.

Proof:

The way the wealthy are taxed falls under something called the *unified transfer tax system (UTTS)*. Under this system, which became valid in 1977, any gifts given to anybody in excess of something called the *annual exclusion amount* (AEA) are subject to gift tax. Basically, what this means is that you can give gifts to an unlimited number of people, up to a certain amount. In 2011, this amount is $13,000. Whether this amount is gifted to one grandchild, three children, or fifteen favorite bellhops, the sums are all a) removed from the donor's estate and b) free of any gift tax.

So what if you give more than that amount? For example, one client gifts her grandchildren $1,000 each year for each digit of their ages. They're nineteen now, so she's gifting $19,000 - $6,000 more than she's allowed to under the AEA.

Well, so what? Pays to be generous, right? Yes—the $13,000 of each gift is being removed from her estate. But what happens to the other $6,000? Under the UTTS, the $6,000 (plus any other gifts in excess of the AEA) are added back into her estate when she dies. Essentially, this means that, if her estate lies above the $5 million mark, her heirs must pay full federal estate tax of 35% on this amount. Say these amounts exceed the threshold. If they do, 35% of $6,000 = $2,100 per gift that she thought she was giving without a consequence. (Well, for her, there isn't any; it's her heirs that are going to have to come up with the cash). And this is only for one year; if she carries on this policy for two grandchildren from age 14 through age 25, the tax rises to over $46,000! That's $4,200 a year to the IRS!

Do you see where this is going? The sooner gift programs begin—at or below the AEA—the more money is removed from the estate, and the less difficulty your heirs will have settling your estate. There will also be less of a chance that they'll have to liquidate assets that may have been in your family for generations (like low cost basis stock or a favorite home).

There's another reason to systematically gift assets; the gift removes the future appreciation of the asset from the donor's estate. In other words, if I had $10,000 worth of Apple stock in 2005, and I gifted it to my nephew, I would remove the 139 shares (at the year-end price) from my estate. In 2005, these 139 shares were worth $10,000. But in 2010, the same 139 shares are worth almost $40,000! I didn't remove $10,000 from my estate; I removed $40,000—and whatever AAPL grows to in the future.

Finally, systematic gifting prevents the greatest enemy to any investment or planning program: procrastination. Setting up an arrangement proactively—rather than waiting for asset returns to distend your estate to a size you never intended it to be—is the best way to ensure that the fruit of your efforts won't be decimated by taxes.

As one additional note, there *are* ways to reduce the size of an estate more rapidly than normal. Among them are gifting 5 years' worth of the AEA at once—per spouse—to a 529 account for the education of a loved one, paying medical or educational institutions directly on behalf of another, or charitable donations. Make sure to check with your attorney and/or planner as to the best ways for you to begin a gifting program.

To do:

- Have your accountant or attorney do an estimate of what your situation would be if you died today. Ask them (most likely this will be the attorney) to explain to you if you're liable to pay gift, estate, or generation-skipping transfer tax.
- If you received a "yes" to any of the answers above, ask them to walk you through the appropriate tax forms for each.
- Ask them what you can do to reduce the size of your estate.

Misconception:

It's safer under the mattress; I don't want my heirs knowing anything.

Reality:

Having at least one other person you trust help you with your wealth usually yields better results than going it alone.

Proof:

You may remember the story of Annat. In June 2009, this Tel Aviv woman decided to surprise her mother for her birthday, so she went to the store and bought her a new mattress. Going one step further, she replaced her old mattress when her mother was away, taking it to the curb. When she realized the switch had occurred, Annat's mother woke up the next morning screaming. Her life savings—$1 million in US dollars and Israeli shekels—was gone for good. CNN's version of the story mentioned that Annat's mother had had "traumatic" experiences with banks.

The story—surreal as a children's cartoon or an episode of the *Twilight Zone*—illustrates all too well that there's nowhere to put wealth without the risk of its loss. In his book *Fundamentals of Financial Planning*, Jeffrey Mershon relates a similar story—namely, the use of safety deposit boxes at the base of metropolitan high-rise buildings.

Specifically, the World Trade Center.

While Mershon notes that this is likely the first time in history that safety deposit boxes with steel reinforcements failed to perform their job in US history, it was simply an example of a risk that was thought to be nonexistent, simply because it had never occurred. But then it did.

It may seem foolish to think all risk can be removed. These two examples are extreme; they don't occur one time in 100,000. But their effects are catastrophic when they do occur.

The common risk with anyone that favors mattresses over banks is much simpler: purchasing power risk. If everything costs more by a factor of 3% every year, that means the mattress is the prime example of an "LMS" investment—one that loses money safely. The reason this type of arrangement is so insidious is that it carries the illusion of protecting your principal. Today it's $100,000, and a year from now it'll still be $100,000. But what you're not realizing, because there's no simple table or chart or news report on it, is that your purchasing power has fallen to $97,000.

Finally, the greatest risk associated with simply sticking it under the mattress and not trusting anyone else is even simpler. What happens if you suffer mental issues, cognitive impairment, or even just forgetfulness? Even for someone with no beneficiaries, no heirs, and no charitable inclinations—the archetype of Ebenezer Scrooge—simply leaving your money in the wall safe for generations hardly seems an adequate estate plan. Even Scrooge at his worst would have left something to Marley's descendants, or to his nephew. Even worse is someone who has heirs they would gladly leave their money to, but just don't trust banks. If a cognitive impairment comes to them, they can greatly impair the financial well-being of their loved ones without even meaning to. And the family members can feel the stress too, especially if they know something's up but can't help their loved one remember. The simplest and most effective estate plans always begin with one step: choose someone to trust.

To do:

- Write down a list of all your family and friends. Review them and try and get an idea of who you trust the most.
- Create a ranking system, either using 1-2-3 or a color coding system. Rank these people, from the ones you trust the most to the ones you trust the least.
- If you have hidden wealth that you haven't told one of your most trusted loved ones about, and you feel you can't, try telling them about a portion of it. Test the result. You may find out telling even a part of your secret lifts a burden from you.

Misconception:

I did my will on nolo.com. All set.

Reality:

While nolo.com is a considerable resource for those without the means to hire an attorney, the complexities inherent in law should create a healthy respect for those who practice it.

Proof:

Let's take a look at what the required reading is for law students at Cornell University. According to lawbooksforless.com, a discount law book site, 32 titles are listed. They are:

| Law 4021—Competition Law and Policy |
| 4121—Gender, Public Policy, and the Law |
| 5001—Civil Procedure |
| 5021—Constitutional Law |
| 5041—Contracts |

5081—Lawyering
5151—Torts
6101—Antitrust Law
6131—Business Organizations
6191—Conflict of Laws
6241—Corporate and White-Collar Crime
6263—Criminal Procedure—Adjudication
6264—Criminal Procedure—Investigations
6441—Federal Income Taxation
6451—Federal Indian Law
6471—Health Law
6561—Intl. Org. and Intl. Human Rights
6731—Dispute Resolution: Negotiation, Mediation, and Arbitration
6752—Persuasive Oral Presentations
6761—Principles of American Legal Writing
6781—Products Liability
6791—Public International law
6801—Remedies in Litigation
6822—Social Science and the Law
6941—Trusts and Estates
7102—Capital Punishment Law
7311—Immigration and Refugee Law
7393—Jurisprudence and Normative Political Theory
7395—Labor and Employment Arbitration
7571—Legal Narratives
7572—Litigation Drafting
7975—Wrongful Conviction and Actual Innocence

If we estimate that each textbook is only 100 pps—a conservative assumption, given the groans of most first-year law students—three years of school requires 3,200 pages of material to study. This is without the lists of cross-references, case precedents, the text of the laws themselves, and historical documents like our own Constitution, the laws of Great Britain, and so on. Finally, this is only the list of titles that were available! From even this cursory look at the material required to produce one attorney—shouldn't it seem evident that nolo.com might be best left as a supplement to a competent attorney specializing in the area you're thinking of?

To do:

- Find out if your area has a bar association. Check this site for help, both by state and county. http://www.romingerlegal.com/natbar. htm
- Go to the front page of nolo: www.nolo.com. Do you see the "Find a Lawyer" box, front and center? This itself is strong evidence that the site knows it can't replace an attorney, but at best act as an adjunct to one.
- If you're an attorney, check the "Get Listed" box at below right! For free, the site will send you a free copy of the book *Deduct It!* (You need a clean bar record and to be accepting new clients.)

WORKS CITED/RECOMMENDED READING

- Mershon, Jeffrey J. *Fundamentals of Personal Financial Planning.* Kaplan, 2006.
- Jr., Winter, Mandell S. *Insurance and Employee Benefits.* Kaplan, 2006.
- Fevurly, Keith R. *Investment Planning.* Kaplan, 2006.
- *Tax Planning.* Kaplan, 2006.
- Mershon, Jeffrey B. *Retirement Planning.* Kaplan, 2006.
- Fevurly, Keith R. *Estate Planning.* Kaplan, 2006.
- Murphy, John J. *Intermarket Analysis: Profiting from Global Market Relationships.* John Wiley & Sons, Hoboken. 2004.
- Edwards, Robert W., Magee, John, and Bassetti, W. H. C. *Technical Analysis of Stock Trends.* BN Publishing, 2008.
- Biggs, Barton. *Hedgehogging.* John Wiley & Sons, Hoboken. 2006.
- Sobel, Robert. *The Great Boom.* St. Martin's Press, New York. 2000.
- Kamenetz, Anya. *Generation Debt: Why now is a terrible time to be young.* Riverhead Books, New York. 2006.
- Nelson, Charles S. *The Investor's Guide to Economic Indicators.* John Wiley & Sons, New York. 1987.
- Levitt, Steven D., and Dubner, Stephen J. *Freakonomics: A Rogue Economist Explores the Hidden Side of Everything.* William Morrow, New York. 2005.
- Knee, Jonathan A. *The Accidental Investment Banker: Inside the Decade that Transformed Wall Street.* Oxford University Press, New York. 2006.
- Harford, Tim. *The Undercover Economist.* Oxford University Press, New York. 2006.

- Landes, David S. *The Wealth and Poverty of Nations: Why Some are so Rich and Some so Poor.* W. W. Norton & Company, New York. 1998.
- Calder, Lendol. *Financing the American Dream; A Cultural History of Consumer Credit.* Princeton University Press, Princeton, NJ. 1999.
- Bucci, Steve. *Credit Repair Kit for Dummies.* Wiley Publishing, Indianapolis. 2006.

JOEL T. REDMOND, CFP ®

CPSIA information can be obtained
at www.ICGtesting.com
Printed in the USA
LVHW090835190322
713862LV00005B/159